STEAM AROUND STAFFORD

MIKE HITCHES

SUTTON PUBLISHING LIMITED

Sutton Publishing Limited
Phoenix Mill · Thrupp · Stroud
Gloucestershire · GL5 2BU

First published 2000

Cover photographs: *Front:* Ex-LMS Stanier
'Jubilee' Class 4–6–0 No. 45672 *Anson* at
Penkridge on the Grand Junction Railway,
which was the first railway route into
Stafford, with a Manchester (London Road)
to Birmingham (New Street) express.
Back: LNWR 'Dreadnought' Compound
2–2–2–0, No. 321 *Servia* resting at Stafford
Station, *c.* 1904.

British Library Cataloguing in Publication Data
A catalogue record for this book is available from the
British Library.

ISBN 0-7509-2368-7

Typeset in 10.5/13.5 Photina.
Typesetting and origination by
Sutton Publishing Limited.
Printed and bound in England
by J.H. Haynes & Co. Ltd, Sparkford.

To Vera

Awaiting its turn of duty is LNWR 'Problem/Lady of the Lake' Class 2–2–2 loco No. 279
Stephenson at the north end of Stafford station, *c.* 1904. (*Roger Carpenter Collection*)

CONTENTS

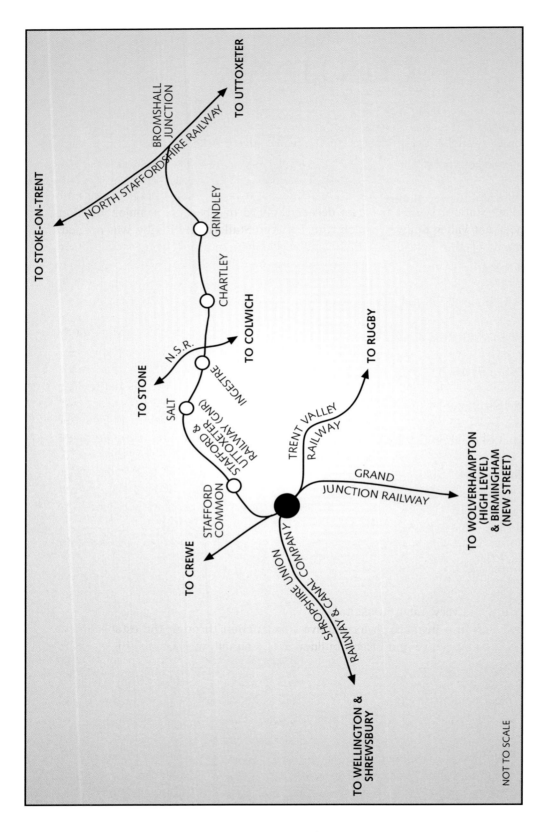

A map showing the routes which have converged on Stafford. (*Author*)

INTRODUCTION

Although Stafford station seems quiet and relatively little used today, it always had an important role in the history of the English railway system. Indeed, the Grand Junction Railway, whose route was the first to reach this county town when opened in 1837, recognized the significance of the town, its most important intermediate station. Within the next decade Stafford had become a major junction when the Trent Valley Railway, which runs between Stafford and Rugby, was opened. Development of this new line, which bypassed the increasingly congested railway network around Birmingham, was the cause of much 'politicking' and 'in-fighting' as competing railway companies vied for control of this key route, the outcome of which was the formation of the mighty London and North Western Railway.

Once conflicts over control of the TVR had been resolved and the new route established, two new branch lines were opened from Stafford. These were the LNWR route to Wellington, which brought the Euston company into conflict with the little, but strong, Shrewsbury and Birmingham Railway who had a shorter route to the Shropshire town from Wolverhampton, Stafford being the focus of this battle. The other branch to open was the Great Northern Railway line between Stafford and Bromshall Junction, where this little line joined the North Staffordshire Railway for access to Uttoxeter and Derby. This line turned out to be the furthest point west reached by the East Coast company over its own metals. The NSR also had a presence in Stafford, its trains running from Stafford, along the GJR to Norton Bridge and thence over its own metals to Stoke-on-Trent. The NSR also met the TVR at Colwich and express trains from Manchester running via Stoke-on-Trent joined the TVR here for the remainder of the journey to Euston.

As Stafford grew in importance, following the opening of new lines, a locoshed was established here to provide motive power for trains operating out of the station. However, its role diminished over the years. Goods facilities were also provided, these being situated in a yard between the station and entrance to the TVR line. This goods yard is still very much in use today.

Stafford was also involved in locomotive construction through the establishment of the private locomotive and wagon builder, W.G. Bagnall, who opened his works in 1875. While the works was no Crewe or Swindon, it played a major role in the economy of the town and provided employment for several hundred men. Its products became world renowned and made Stafford famous as a centre for locomotive building and railway engineering.

Over the years the railway and station at Stafford have been the centre of many changes including those of ownership, not least the complete renewal of the station as part of the electrification of the West Coast Main Line in the 1960s. Its branches were closed in the middle of the twentieth century, along with the locoshed, and Bagnall's locoworks has also disappeared. However, as the station and the TVR are on or part of the main line between Glasgow and London (Euston), they have seen top link express locos from famous LNWR locos, Stafford being the border between the Northern and Southern divisions of the Euston company, with locos being changed here until such duties were moved to Crewe, through to the mighty LMS and BR Pacific engines. Nowadays, fast electric trains race through Stafford on their way to Euston, Scotland and Birmingham, although some express services still call at the station. An infrequent local service between Stafford and Coventry is still operating, using Diesel Multiple Unit trains, but many others have disappeared from the timetable. All a far cry from the days of steam when famous locos were seen at Stafford.

To the travelling public Stafford is just somewhere that is passed through on the way to more exotic destinations, if places like London and Birmingham can be so called, which seems rather unfair. In preparing this work, therefore, I hope that I have been able to redress the balance and have managed to illustrate just how important Stafford and its railways have been in the history of Britain's railway system and the key role it still plays as a major junction today.

ACKNOWLEDGEMENTS

I should like to express my grateful thanks to all of those organizations and individuals who have helped in putting this work together. Those organisations whose assistance was invaluable include the County Record Office, Stafford, the library at University of Wales, Bangor, and the *Wolverhampton Express* and *Star*.

Individual assistance was provided by David Ibbotson, Arthur Truby, Allan C. Baker, Chris Hawkins, Roger Carpenter and F.W. 'Tim' Shuttleworth. I would also like to thank Glad Stockdale for her excellent work on the maps. Special thanks go to the late Jim Pearson who provided valuable assistance and material on the history of the Bagnall locoworks. Without his help the story of the company would have been impossible to complete. Finally, my thanks go to Hilary and Gary, whose support is always a welcome source of inspiration.

CHAPTER ONE

THE GRAND JUNCTION RAILWAY

Stafford was established on the railway map following construction of the Grand Junction Railway, the company feeling that the county town was important enough to warrant siting of a railway station here. Given Royal Assent on 6 May 1833, the GJR was to run from Birmingham to Earlestown (then known as Newton Junction) where it joined the Liverpool and Manchester Railway, giving access to these two important Lancashire towns. The L&M had opened in 1830 and was a very successful venture, making a profit of £14,432 in its first three months of operation. The L&M was the inspiration for development of the GJR and London and Birmingham Railway, both of which were authorized on the same day. These two new companies were established to provide a railway link between England's capital city, the major seaport at Liverpool and the cotton capital of Manchester. Birmingham, which was a rapidly expanding West Midlands industrial town, was to become the interchange point between the GJR and the London & Birmingham Railway.

George Stephenson was appointed Engineer for construction of the GJR and he was assisted by another great railway engineer, Joseph Locke. It was Locke, however, owing to a disagreement with Stephenson, who took actual responsibility for building the line, including all earthworks, viaducts and station buildings. Locke built a double track railway, using double sided iron rails of his own invention, so that they could be turned over when worn. Unfortunately, as iron is soft, the undersides became dented where they pressed into the chairs and could not be turned over. The GJR was cheap to construct, the only major engineering work being a twenty-arch viaduct over the River Weaver, and cost £18,846 a mile to build. Major stopping places were at Warrington (where trains operating to and from Liverpool and Manchester were divided or joined), Hartford, Crewe (where the GJR established a locoworks after 1843), Whitmore (where locos were watered), Stafford and Wolverhampton.

At Stafford, land registered for use of the GJR was situated in the parish of St Mary's and included a house and yard owned by John Milner, along with a 'pleasure ground' and orchard, blacksmith's shop and garden, pasture, stable and two gardens belonging to Charles Read, a mill pool, silk factory, two meadows, three arable fields, one plantation, one meadow and stable all owned by John Milner. The line was then to cross a river dividing Weston from Chebsey, owned by the Earl of Lichfield. No doubt acquisition of this land added substantial costs to the construction of the line.

Opening of the GJR took place on Tuesday 4 July 1837, the first train leaving Birmingham at 7 a.m., hauled by locomotive *Wildfire*, and was made up of eight

On Saturday 16 June 1951, ex-LMS Stanier 'Jubilee' Class No. 45588 *Kashmir* heads a London to Blackpool train, reporting number W99, on the Down fast line at Great Bridgeford, north of Stafford, on the GJR, the first railway route to include Stafford on its map. The train has the reporting number W99 on the smokebox door and is probably an excursion train for the North Wales coast as the train was photographed on 16 June 1951. (*P. Kendrick; F.W. Shuttleworth Collection*)

coaches. The first train from Liverpool left Lime Street station at 6.30 a.m. and was rope hauled through tunnels and up the bank. Having arrived at the top of the bank, loco *Dr Dainton* took the train to Warrington, where the three coaches from Manchester were attached for the remainder of the journey to Birmingham, *Dr Dainton* remaining in charge. While the opening of the GJR was a rather low-key affair, at Stafford, which was the most important intermediate station on the route, celebrations were very much greater. When *Wildfire* approached Stafford, from Birmingham, the Mayor fired a 21-gun salute, using an ancient cannon, and a massive crowd thronged the station to witness such a monumental event. Vast crowds also lined the track leading into Stafford to witness the arrival of the first train. These first trains also carried mail coaches, the Post Office recognizing the importance of the new railways in the transit of mail, and arranging for collection of mail from towns close to the line. The GJR assumed a more important role when the L&B opened a year later and a full connection to London was made.

On 16 June 1951, ex-LMS un-named 'Patriot' Class 4–6–0 No. 45510, in green livery, approaches Great Bridgeford on the Up fast line with the second part of the W98 Glasgow–Birmingham train, made up of fourteen corridor coaches. The reporting number, W98, identifies the train, the /2 indicates that the service had been duplicated due to heavy demand and that this train is the second of the two provided. The divergence of the fast and slow lines is due to the island platform shown in the photograph on page 8. The station was closed to passengers on 8 August 1949. (*P. Kendrick; F.W. Shuttleworth Collection*)

Ex-LMS Class 5 4–6–0 No. 44971, with self-weighting tender, is on the Up slow line as it approaches Great Bridgeford with a nine-coach train of both corridor and non-corridor stock bound for Birmingham (New Street) on 4 August 1951. (*P. Kendrick; F.W. Shuttleworth Collection*)

Ex-LNWR 3P 'Experiment' Class 4–6–0 as LMS No. 25473 *Scottish Chief* is leaving Stafford, taking the GJR line as it heads an Up express to Birmingham (New Street). The TVR line can be seen curving away in the background with Stafford No. 1 signal-box, which controls the junction, visible behind the train. An unidentified Class 4P 4–6–2 tank engine can be seen on the right in Rickerscote loop. This scene was photographed in about 1934. As an important stopping place Stafford was provided with a station which had platforms for both Up and Down lines, each with its own buildings providing all necessary facilities. The main building was on the Up (Birmingham) platform and had a 'grand entrance' of twin classical columns which supported a semi-circular arched window surround, all designed to give an impression of confidence in this new form of transport. A smaller version of the main building was provided on the Down (Crewe) platform. Once the GJR began operating Stafford station was served by six trains a day, which took 1 hour 20 minutes for the journey to Birmingham and 3 hours 45 minutes to Liverpool. The fare to Birmingham was 6*s* first class and 4*s* 6*d* second class. The fare to Liverpool was 14*s* 6*d* first class and 10*s* second class. (*P. Kendrick; F.W. Shuttleworth Collection*)

The Down platform at Gailey station, on the GJR between Stafford and Wolverhampton, on 16 June 1951, the last day of passenger service. (*P. Kendrick; F.W. Shuttleworth Collection*)

Travelling on the new GJR was a novel experience for passengers and one C.S. Greaves of Stafford wrote in a letter of 11 July 1837:

> I came fleeting from Worc's to Birmingham and thence by the Railway further, bringing the carriage I have tried with me on the Railway. The travelling in this way is such a novelty that I shall endeavour to describe it. First of all is the steam engine with the place for the coals behind it neither of which are capable of description – Then follows carriages chained to each other, and within about a yard of each other. The place in which I sat contained 6–3 with their faces towards the engine, 3 the contrary way – I should say it is about 6 feet broad by four wide. Each passenger sits in a sort of armed chair – The two nearest the entrance having that to lean against and there being arms coming out of a junction intervening between each passenger this projection goes up to the top and is stuffed and soft. I can just sit in the middle seat, and there is plenty of leg room as I think it is about a foot from my knee to the opposite seat. There is a door and window on each side like a commercial coach, but larger and much more commodious for passengers in and out. The carriage is very handsomely fitted up. The only thing that I thought was that it appeared that the windows are hardly sufficient. The same coach certainly contains other seats and I think, but I cannot say for certain, 3 before and 3 behind so that each contains 12 persons. 7 coaches came with us therefore there were about 84 passengers. The pace is very steady, regular, and never apparently too fast, yet we came from B'ham to here, 30 miles, in an hour and five minutes. Excluding 7 minutes lost at Wolverhampton and from that place 16 miles in 28 minutes – At present I am clear the rails are not properly settled, as in some places you clearly experience a jar at each junction, and in others a lateral movement. The only thing in which I was deceived was the quality of the motion, which at present is much greater than I expected, but I was convinced will ultimately be avoided nearly altogether. It certainly is a delightful method of getting over the ground and no one I should think having once travelled by it would ever trouble horses again if he could avoid it. The noise of the engine is by no means discomforting – You may almost fancy it the quick galloping of horses – You see but little of the country partly by reason of the rapidity, but chiefly owing to the low level of the rails, which in many places almost touches the brooks they pass. It is in vain to try to catch the features of the person you pass – and only curious to see how the arches you go under appear magnificent in size. The seats and tickets being all numbered there is little confusion about places and the luggage is piled on the tops of the vehicles. I have no doubt many improvements may still be made, but I think it is good enough as it is. If you have a carriage you may ride in that. James did so all the way. It is I believe 110 miles from B'ham to L'pool – including stoppages 4½ hours. A capital means of transmitting a family any distance in a day.

Clearly Mr Greaves enjoyed his journey to Stafford and he was aware of potential improvements. What, I wonder, would he have made of today's fast electric railway? Indeed, would he have thought it an improvement at all?

Mrs Rooke, the stationmistress at Gailey station, superintends the departure of the 2.39 p.m. Birmingham train on the last day of the passenger service, 16 June 1951. The train, the 12.40 from Manchester (London Road), had travelled via Stoke-on-Trent and consisted of seven corridor carriages headed by 'Patriot' Class No. 45520 *Llandudno*, which later in the day hauled the last northbound train to call at Gailey. (*P. Kendrick; F.W. Shuttleworth Collection*)

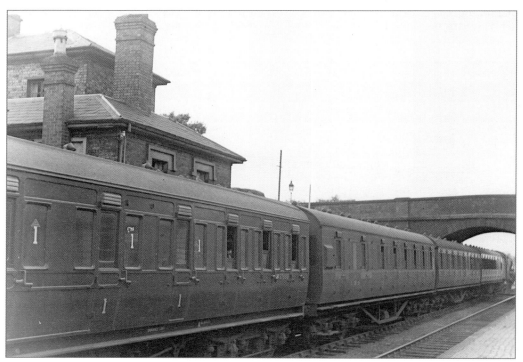

The last train to call at Gailey station, 7.06 p.m., 16 June 1951. This train, made up of four non-corridor carriages hauled by 'Patriot' Class No. 45520 *Llandudno*, was the 5.57 p.m. from Birmingham (New Street) to Stoke-on-Trent, which called at every station *en route* except for Winson Green and Wedgwood Halt. (*P. Kendrick; F.W. Shuttleworth Collection*)

Ex-LMS Class 2P 4–4–0 No. 40660, of Crewe North shed, hauls the Crewe Civil Engineer's inspection saloon No. M45029M, in early BR carmine and cream livery, on the Down slow line at Stableford, between Standon Bridge and Whitmore, on 20 April 1955. (*P. Kendrick; F.W. Shuttleworth Collection*)

Ten days later, on 30 April 1955, at the same location, former MR Class 3F 0–6–0 No. 43623, of Burton-on-Trent shed, hauls a northbound loose-coupled goods train. (*P. Kendrick; F.W. Shuttleworth Collection*)

CHAPTER TWO

THE TRENT VALLEY RAILWAY

Secretary of the GJR was the autocratic and devious Captain Mark Huish. His 'wheeler-dealing' brought about the formation of the mighty LNWR in 1846, Stafford becoming the boundary point between the Northern and Southern Divisions, on formation of the new company. Stafford itself was indirectly involved in Huish's campaign to protect the interests of the GJR early in 1845, when he revealed just how devious he could be.

In that year relations between the GJR and the L&B became extremely frosty when Huish discovered that the L&B was interested in the activities of the Manchester and Birmingham Railway, which appeared to isolate the GJR by depriving it of traffic to the north-west. Suspicions were further aroused when the L&B took an interest in the independent TVR, whose projected 45-mile line would avoid Birmingham altogether and make the L&B independent of the GJR in Birmingham. The TVR was planned to leave the L&B at Rugby and join the GJR at Stafford (where interchange of traffic between the L&B and GJR could take place). The projected route was destined to make Stafford one of the more important junctions on the still infant railway network.

Alarmed by what he viewed as treachery on the part of the L&B, Huish sought co-operation of the broad gauge Great Western Railway to build a line of their own from the GJR terminus in Birmingham to join the Oxford branch of the GWR, opened in 1844. This project was supported by industrialists in Birmingham who were not happy with the L&B's alleged abuse of its monopoly, especially in its conduct over goods traffic, with a tendency to charge extortionate rates and a refusal to supply much needed additional accommodation. Directors of the GWR on the other hand, resisted approaches from the GJR for some time, until hostility of the L&B over that company's plans to build a railway from Rugby to Oxford, together with efforts being made by the Midland Railway to force the broad gauge out of Gloucester and Bristol by purchasing the Birmingham and Bristol Railway from under the nose of the GWR (making transfer of passengers and freight between the two gauges as difficult as possible), led the GWR to believe that no friendly interchange of traffic was possible. Once the GWR was convinced of hostility by other railway companies it gave full support to the new project, which was planned to be broad gauge. The GJR even went as far as proposing to add broad gauge rails on their own routes to Liverpool and Manchester, giving the GWR access to the lucrative traffic from these great north-western cities. Estimates of the cost of adding the broad gauge were made by the GJR Engineer as a sign of good faith.

What the GWR were unaware of, however, was that Huish was set on a ploy to bring the L&B, M&B and TVR around the negotiating table. He did this by announcing that bringing the broad gauge into Rugby would 'avoid all curses of monopoly', creating some alarm to the L&B who were determined that the 4 ft 8½ in gauge should be adopted as standard at the expense of the 7 ft 0¼ in of the GWR. In the event problems concerning the TVR were resolved when the GJR provided capital to build the line in exchange for full running powers. Under such circumstances, the L&B had little choice but to come to terms with the GJR who, in turn, deserted the GWR having no further need to compete with the L&B. Further, Huish – who appeared to be anti-monopoly when in dispute with the L&B – was now very keen to maintain a monopoly when it suited his purposes, and the GWR was to find itself up against an implacable enemy who would attempt to block any effort made by the Paddington company to gain access to his north-western territories.

The Trent Valley line was completed and opened in December 1847, only a year after friendly relations between the old protagonists had been so good that they were merged on 16 July 1846 to form the LNWR, later destined to become the largest joint stock company in the world, with Captain Mark Huish as General Manager.

At the head of a Down express is ex-LNWR 'Claughton' Class 4–6–0 as LMS No. 5918 *Frederick Baynes*, just north of Rugeley, on the Trent Valley Railway as it heads towards Stafford, *c.* 1934. (*P. Kendrick; F.W. Shuttleworth Collection*)

The TVR junction, looking from the Wolverhampton Road bridge, just south of Stafford station, *c.* 1905. Just about to enter the tightly curved Queensville Curve, which placed a 10 mph speed limit on all trains, is LNWR Webb three-cylinder compound loco on the Up fast line, as it heads a London-bound express. A Down train is approaching Stafford from Birmingham on the GJR line. It is probably a goods train as it is signalled for the Down slow line. On the TVR the fast lines were in the centre, flanked by slow lines on either side with connections to the goods yards. An early attempt was made by the embryonic M&B to build a line through the Trent Valley; its projected 8-mile route was to run from Stone to Colwich and was promoted in 1839 as a route to London which would be independent of the GJR. Although the scheme failed to gain parliamentary approval, a line through the Trent Valley which avoided Birmingham was kept alive by local businessmen, and an independent company was formed in 1843. Two years after, arrangements were made for the L&B to lease the line, which was to run between Stafford and Rugby. It was this arrangement which so alarmed Captain Mark Huish, Secretary of the GJR. Along with GJR plans to involve the GWR in a rival route, Huish also managed to obtain authority to subscribe a large amount of capital to the TVR project in exchange for full running powers, made under the Trent Valley Authorization Act of 1845, Royal Assent being given on 21 July. The Act provided for a capital investment of £1,250,000 in £20 shares, and there was also provision to raise a loan capital of £416,000. The first sod was cut at Camel Close, ½ mile from Tamworth, in the following November, by Prime Minister Sir Robert Peel, MP for Tamworth. In April 1846, the TVR Company was bought outright by the L&B, GJR and M&B, and construction was well under way when the LNWR was formed. The railway's engineers were Robert Stephenson and George Bidder, with T.L. Gooch in charge. The contractor was Thomas Brassey, who had already been involved in many railway contracts. On completion, the new line was scheduled to open on 26 June 1847, and a celebration was held in Tamworth. A special train from Euston to Rugby brought guests, where a MR train, carrying 'Railway King' George Hudson was waiting with another special train from Birmingham. The whole party then proceeded along the new line to Tamworth. It is believed that the 'Railway King' behaved rather badly during the event. Opening celebrations proved premature as concern had been expressed over six cast-iron bridges, which were similar to one which had collapsed over the River Dee at Chester in May 1847, bringing down a train. Although the line inspector, Captain Joshua Coddington, was happy to allow opening of the new line, the government was studying the use of cast-iron bridges and a further inspection was requested which allowed opening, so that goods trains – along with two local trains – began operations from 15 September 1847. The route, however, was not to be fully used until the beginning of December. (*F.W. Shuttleworth Collection*)

Ex-LMS Stanier Class 2–6–4T No. 42585, of Rugby shed, pauses in a siding at Milford and Brocton station with the Northampton District Engineer's saloon, No. M45039M, on 29 August 1956. The engine had propelled the vehicle from Northampton. (*P. Kendrick; F.W. Shuttleworth Collection*)

A further view, on 29 August 1956, of the inspection train at Milford and Brocton, which was the northern extremity of the Northampton District Engineer's territory. The saloon, No. M45039M, was built by the Lancashire & Yorkshire Railway as long ago as 1885; note the quilted leather padding on the inside of the open door. (*P. Kendrick; F.W. Shuttleworth Collection*)

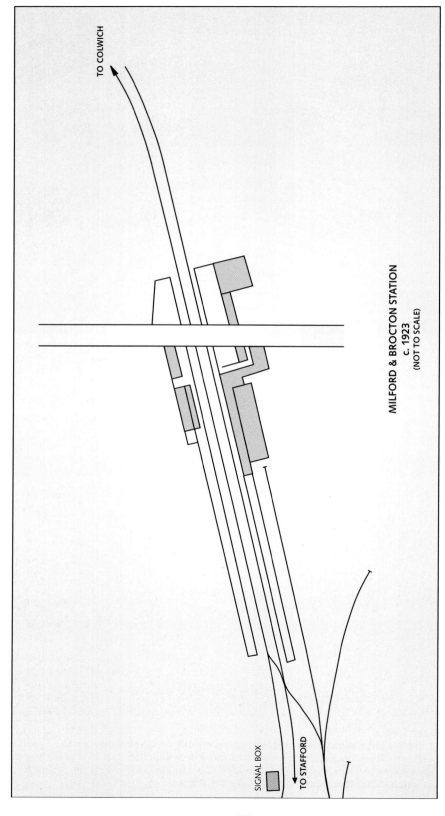

MILFORD & BROCTON STATION
c. 1923
(NOT TO SCALE)

TO COLWICH

TO STAFFORD

SIGNAL BOX

A plan of Milford and Brocton station, the first on the Trent Valley Railway after leaving Stafford, *c.* 1923. (*Author*)

Milford and Brocton station, opened on 18 May 1877, looking south towards Shugborough Tunnel from the Down platform, *c.* 1900. The bridge, seen crossing the line, is a road bridge which gave access to the short wooden platforms of the station. The station buildings were also constructed in timber and were single-storey affairs of simple design. A small goods siding was also provided behind the Down platform. The line between here and Stafford was quadrupled in 1898, opening on 26 July, and widening became necessary on the TVR to accommodate trains running over the route. This was the most important route for expresses between Euston and the north-west of England, Scotland and North Wales, which avoided Birmingham and cut distance between London and the north. (*Author's Collection*)

Railway cottages built by the LNWR for station staff at Milford and Brocton, as they appeared in 1974. These houses, like many on the LNWR, were built of brick made in the company's brickworks at Crewe. Therefore Crewe not only undertook loco building, but also made the bricks which built homes for the Euston company's workers. The station itself closed on 6 March 1950 but freight was still handled there until March 1960. (*D. Ibbotson*)

LMS 'Turbomotive' Pacific No. 6202, emerging from Shugborough Tunnel at the head of a Liverpool–Euston express on 20 July 1937. Shugborough Tunnel follows almost immediately after Milford and Brocton station. This 774-yd long tunnel was the only major engineering feature on the whole of the TVR, and its flamboyant portals earned it the nickname 'The Gates of Jerusalem'. (P. Kendrick; F.W. Shuttleworth Collection)

The north end of Shugborough Tunnel with LMS Class 4F 0–6–0 No. 4198 emerging at the head of a Down local train for Stafford in July 1937. The 'Gates of Jerusalem' epithet can be judged in this view. (P. Kendrick; F.W. Shuttleworth Collection)

Colwich station, as it appeared at the turn of the twentieth century. Situated some 3½ miles from Milford and Brocton, Colwich was one of the original stations when the TVR opened. The twin pavilioned buildings seen here replaced the original Jacobean station building, which was retained as the stationmaster's house, when rebuilt in 1871. Colwich was the most northerly of five junctions on the TVR and the station was shared with the NSR, whose line from Stone was opened on 1 May 1849 and joined the TVR beside the Trent and Mersey canal. This line was also important to the LNWR who, thanks to the NSR Act of 13 August 1849, had running powers over the Stoke company's metals to Manchester. Although providing a shorter route, the existence of Harecastle Tunnel limited size of motive power and the line was not fully exploited until 1960s electrification. The LNWR/LMS operated Euston–Manchester (London Road) expresses over the line, thereby by-passing Stafford, the most famous of these being 'The Comet'. (*Author's Collection*)

Ex-NSR 'New M' Class 0–4–4 tank, as LMS No. 1436 awaits departure from Colwich, with an early morning local passenger train from Walsall to Stoke-on-Trent, August 1935. Local services between Colwich and Stoke-on-Trent ceased during the coal shortage of 1947 and never returned. Colwich station itself was closed on 14 September 1957. (*P. Kendrick; F.W. Shuttleworth Collection*)

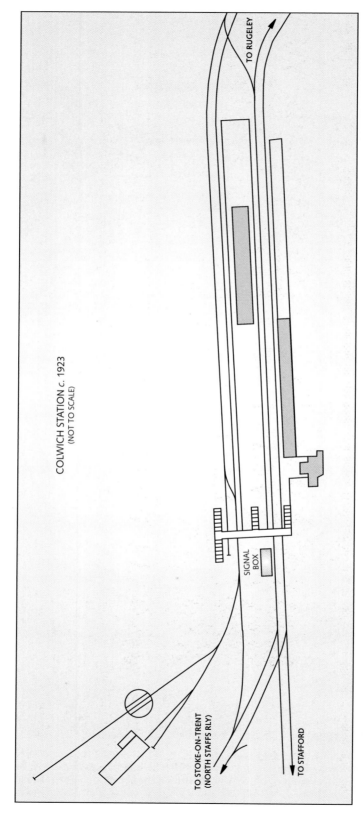

COLWICH STATION c. 1923
(NOT TO SCALE)

TO RUGELEY

SIGNAL BOX

TO STOKE-ON-TRENT (NORTH STAFFS RLY)

TO STAFFORD

A plan of Colwich station, c. 1923. The plan shown here is of the station which was rebuilt by the LNWR in 1871 to coincide with widening to four tracks of the TVR at this point. (*Author*)

ex-LNWR 'Prince of Wales' Class 4–6–0 No. 25658 heads a Down express along the TVR, towards Stafford, mid-1930s. (*P. Kendrick; F.W. Shuttleworth Collection*)

Just north of Rugeley on the TVR is a local train, headed by ex-LNWR 2–4–2 tank No. 6666, passing an unidentified ex-LNWR 0–8–0 heavy-freight engine, mid-1930s. The quadrupled track was built in the 1870s as demand on the TVR exceeded capacity to cope with trains then running over the route. (*P. Kendrick; F.W. Shuttleworth Collection*)

Ex-LNWR 0–8–0, as LMS No. 9348, heads a mixed freight train along the TVR just north of Rugeley in the mid-1930s. These freight locos were a common sight on the route, hauling heavy freight trains right up to the end of the 1950s. The locosheds at Rugby, Nuneaton and Stafford always had an allocation of them for such work. (*P. Kendrick; F.W. Shuttleworth Collection*)

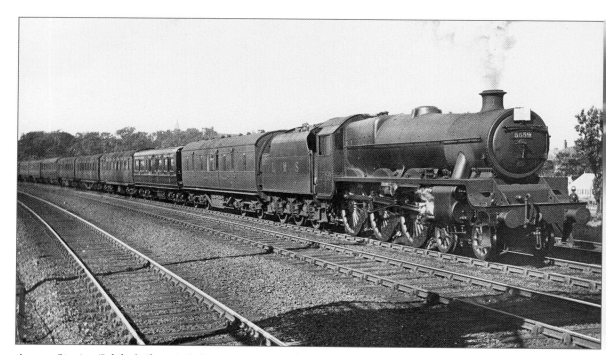

A new Stanier 'Jubilee' Class 4–6–0, as yet unnamed, No. 5559 heads a Down express towards Stafford, seen here north of Rugeley, *c.* 1936. The engine was later to be named *British Columbia*. (*P. Kendrick; F.W. Shuttleworth Collection*)

LMS Stanier 'Jubilee' Class 4–6–0 No. 5586 *Mysore* heads a fitted freight train along the TVR, north of Rugeley, late 1930s. (*P. Kendrick; F.W. Shuttleworth Collection*)

Unnamed LMS 'Jubilee' Class 4–6–0 No. 5613 with Stanier high-sided tender heads a northbound express up the TVR, just north of Rugeley, mid-1930s. The engine would later be named *Kenya*. (*P. Kendrick; F.W. Shuttleworth Collection*)

LMS 'Jubilee' Class 4–6–0 No. 5691 *Orion* and an unidentified LMS 'Royal Scot' Class 4–6–0 head a northbound express up the TVR, mid-1930s. (*P. Kendrick; F.W. Shuttleworth Collection*)

A local train heads along the Down fast line north of Rugeley, headed by LMS Fowler 2–6–2 tank No. 53, mid-1930s. (*P. Kendrick; F.W. Shuttleworth Collection*)

train of non-corridor stock heads along the TVR, just north of Rugeley towards Stafford, headed by LMS
anier 2–6–2 tank No. 101, *c.* 1935. (*P. Kendrick; F.W. Shuttleworth Collection*)

MS Stanier 2–6–2 tank loco appears to be resting on the Down slow line, north of Rugeley, *c.* 1935. The
hedcode plate 5C, on the smokebox door, indicates that the engine is allocated to Stafford. (*P. Kendrick;
W. Shuttleworth Collection*)

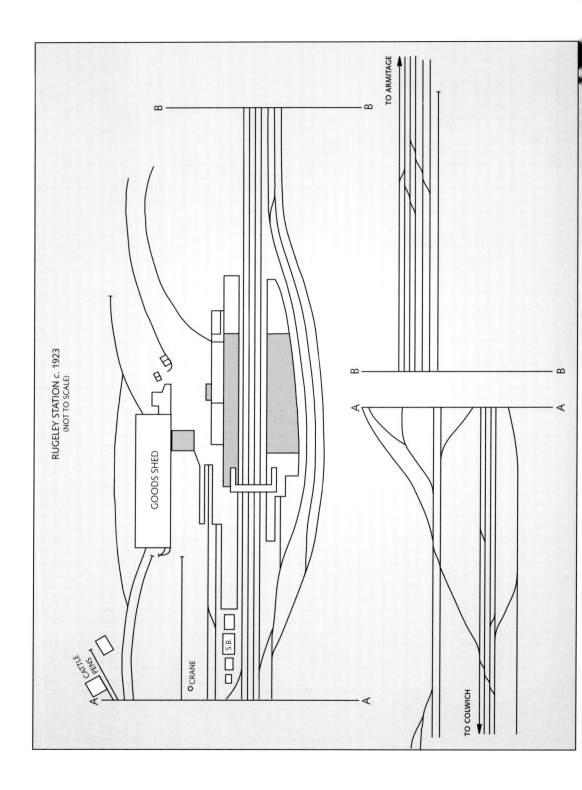

RUGELEY STATION c. 1923
(NOT TO SCALE)

CATTLE
PENS

CRANE

GOODS SHED

S.B.

TO ARMITAGE

TO COLWICH

Rugeley station, another of the original TVR stations, at the end of the nineteenth century. Its Jacobean-style main building, just visible at the south end of the Up platform, was designed by John Livock who was responsible for the architecture of all the original eleven stations on the route. Until the line closed in 1965, Rugeley was a junction station for the South Staffordshire Railway route for Hednesford and Walsall, which served the Cannock coalfields and provided a number of coal trains that ran along the TVR. The name 'Rugeley' derives from the colour of the native rocks. Rugeley itself was the centre for manufacturing Jeweller's Rouge, used in the polishing of gemstones, much of this material finding its way to places like the 'Jewellery Quarter' in Birmingham and Hatton Garden, London. In the 1850s, residents of Rugeley wanted to change the name of the town and sent a deputation to the then Prime Minister, Palmerston, for permission to do this. The Prime Minister was not in favour of a change but suggested, in a fit of humour, that the town be called 'Palmerston' after himself. This suggestion, however, brought to mind unfortunate associations with one Dr Palmer, an infamous murderer who poisoned his wealthy patients by use of strychnine, and who had committed his crimes while resident in the town. Needless to say, therefore, the name change idea was quickly forgotten. The station is still open today, although the goods sidings and yards, like many on the TVR, were removed when the line was electrified in the 1960s. (*Author's Collection*)

An ex-LNWR 0–6–0 No. 8352 heads a local train out of Rugeley, as it heads for the SSR line to Hednesford, early 1930s. (*P. Kendrick; F.W. Shuttleworth Collection*)

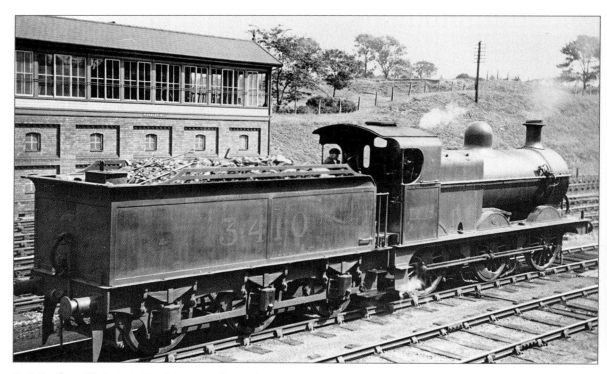

Ex-MR Class 3F 0–6–0 No. 3410 stands on the Down line for Hednesford, close to Rugeley No. 1 signal-box, *c.* 1930. The engine, No. 3410, was allocated to Walsall, where it remained for many years. (*P. Kendrick; F.W. Shuttleworth Collection*)

Ex-LNWR 0–8–0 heavy freight engine, as LMS No. 9031, is coming off the line from Hednesford with a coal train from Cannock Chase pits, in April 1947, less than a year before the railways were nationalized by the new post-war Labour government. (*P. Kendrick; F.W. Shuttleworth Collection*)

Ex-LNWR 2–4–2 'Passenger Tank', as LMS No. 6637, is seen leaving the TVR at Rugeley with a local train for Hednesford in the late 1920s. The MR-style numbers can be seen on the tank sides of the loco, while the new LMS crest, which would be dropped on locos in the 1930s in favour of the company's initials, is visible on the coal bunker sides. (*P. Kendrick; F.W. Shuttleworth Collection*)

An Up Trent Valley local passenger train is standing at Rugeley station, 1930s. The loco in this view is a Bowen-Cooke 'Superheater Tank' 4–6–2, as LMS No. 6992, and was allocated to Stafford shed at the time. At this date, MR-style numbering was still in use, but the company's crest had been replaced by LMS lettering. (*P. Kendrick; F.W. Shuttleworth Collection*)

An ex-MR 3F 0–6–0 heads a local train from Rugeley station towards the branch to Hednesford, early 1930s. The 1923 'Grouping' brought an influx of ex-MR locomotive types to this previously LNWR line, as the new LMS had a strong Midland influence in the early years of its existence. (*P. Kendrick; F.W. Shuttleworth Collection*)

A broadside view of an ex-LNWR 4–4–0 loco, as LMS No. 5126 *Dominion*, at Rugeley station, late 1920s. The LMS crest is clearly visible here. (*P. Kendrick; F.W. Shuttleworth Collection*)

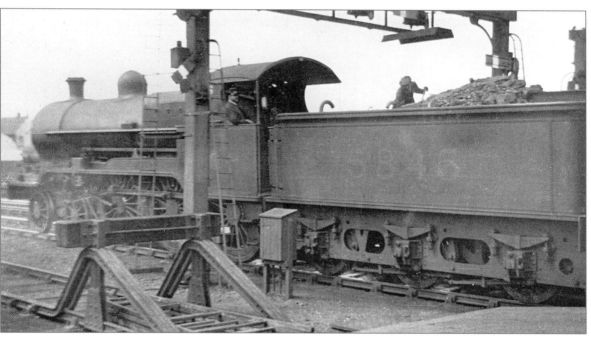

'Prince of Wales' Class 4–6–0, as LMS No. 5845, is waiting at Rugeley station with a Down express, late 1920s. The fireman is busy moving coal forward on the tender, while the driver awaits the signal from the guard to depart. LMS No. 5845, although mainly of LNWR design, was built by Beardsmore in 1924 for the LMS and was the only 'Prince of Wales' Class engine to be built with Walschaerts valve gear and raised running plate (although 964 *Bret Harte* had been so converted following the Betley Road accident in which engine No. 1335 broke a connecting rod while hauling a heavy Down Manchester express at 65–70 mph; subsequently three other 'Prince' Class engines were also converted). LMS No. 5845, resplendent in LMS crimson lake livery, was exhibited at the 1924 Wembley Exhibition where it temporarily carried the nameplates *Prince of Wales* in honour of the president of the exhibition. An example of the standard 'Prince of Wales' Class engine, with Joy valve gear, is shown on page 23. The enginemen promptly christened the five Walschaerts valve gear engines 'Tishies' after a well-known racehorse which had the peculiar habit of crossing its legs and falling over when apparently well set to win a race. (*P. Kendrick; F.W. Shuttleworth Collection*)

Approaching Rugeley station with a Down express is LMS Class 4P Compound 4–4–0 No. 1154, mid-1930s. On the left of the picture is Rugeley No. 1 signal-box and on the right is the entrance to the branch for Rugeley Town, Hednesford and Walsall. (*P. Kendrick; F.W. Shuttleworth Collection*)

Passing Rugeley No. 2 signal-box is ex-LMS 'Crab' 2–6–0, as British Railways No. 42920, with an Up fitted freight train, 1959. The passenger footbridge can be seen in this view and the goods yard, on the right, still appears to be busy with plenty of freight traffic. (*Roger Carpenter*)

One of the BR 'Britannia' Class Pacifics, No. 70031 *Byron* hauls the Down 'Mancunian' through Rugeley station, 1956. (*Roger Carpenter*)

The SSR had its own station at Rugeley, which opened on 1 June 1870 and was the source of hopeless confusion between station names in the town. The SSR station was known as Rugeley (Trent Valley) in branch timetables, while the station on the main TVR was known simply as Rugeley. This confusion was only resolved during the First World War, when it was laid down that Rugeley (Trent Valley) was the only name for the station on the TVR route, this ruling being effective from 15 April 1917. The SSR station, by then under LNWR control, was retitled Rugeley Town. Rugeley Town station is seen here in the 1920s. (*Author's Collection*)

Some 3¼ miles from Rugeley is Armitage station, with an LNWR train departing, early 1900s. This was another of the original eleven stations at the opening of the TVR. Although the station buildings are of timber, as this was only a secondary stopping place, it was designed by John Livock. The station served a sanitary pottery works, Armitage Ware (now Armitage Shanks), which has become famous for its toilets, baths and washbasins the world over. The pottery works here led to the construction of a goods station at Armitage, which was opened on 1 October 1877. Armitage station was officially closed on 13 June 1960, as the TVR was prepared for electrification. However, the last trains to call at Armitage were on Saturday 11 June, the station not then being served by Sunday trains. (*Author's Collection*)

Opposite: An Up express, hauled by an unidentified LMS 'Royal Scot' Class 4–6–0, passes by a signal gantry controlling the Down lines just south of Rugeley, late 1930s. Just visible on the left is the branch to Hednesford. (*The late Eric S. Russell; collection of F.W. Shuttleworth*)

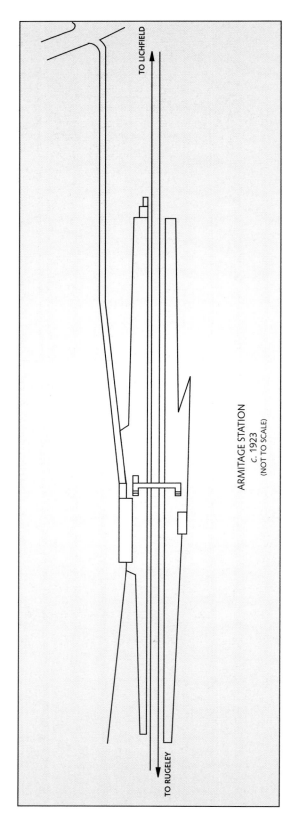

ARMITAGE STATION
c. 1923
(NOT TO SCALE)

TO LICHFIELD

TO RUGELEY

A plan of the simple layout at Armitage station, c. 1923. (*Author*)

Ex-LMS rebuilt 'Patriot' Class 4–6–0 No. 45540 *Sir Richard Turnbull* passes through Lichfield (Trent Valley) station with the Down 'Comet' express for Manchester (London Road), *c.* 1956. The train would then leave the TVR at Colwich and run to Manchester via Stoke-on-Trent. Lichfield (Trent Valley) station lay some 4⅜ miles from Armitage and was an original TVR station. This was one of three designated by the TVR company as a 'First Class' station, and the John Livock-designed buildings were substantial, with a Jacobean style. Just south of the station, the SSR line between Birmingham and Derby crossed the TVR; its station, Lichfield City, now Lichfield (Trent Valley) High Level, still has a train service, terminus of the 'Cross-City' line from Redditch, Longbridge, Birmingham (New Street), and Sutton Coldfield. (*Roger Carpenter*)

At the head of the Down 'Comet' is BR 'Britannia' Pacific No. 70033 *Charles Dickens*, passing through Lichfield (Trent Valley) station in 1955. Lichfield is famous for its three-spired cathedral and as the birthplace of Dr Samuel Johnson. Other famous inhabitants of the city have included David Garrick and Anna Sewell, author of *Black Beauty*. (*Roger Carpenter*)

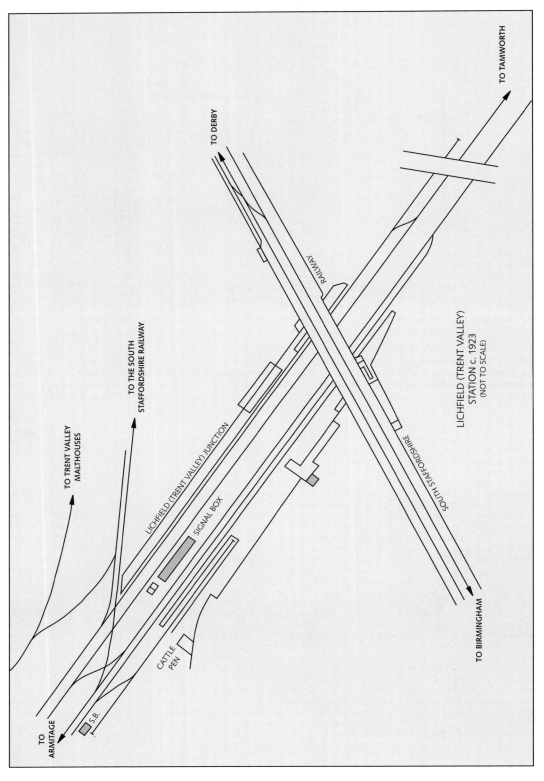

TO ARMITAGE

S.B.

TO TRENT VALLEY MALTHOUSES

TO THE SOUTH STAFFORDSHIRE RAILWAY

LICHFIELD (TRENT VALLEY) JUNCTION

SIGNAL BOX

CATTLE PEN

TO DERBY

RAILWAY

SOUTH STAFFORDSHIRE

TO TAMWORTH

TO BIRMINGHAM

LICHFIELD (TRENT VALLEY)
STATION c. 1923
(NOT TO SCALE)

A plan of the station of Lichfield (Trent Valley), c. 1923. Also visible is the SSR line, which crosses the TVR here, between Birmingham and Derby, with Lichfield City station in view, along with the TVR junction to the SSR to the north of the station. Also to the north of the station there was a line to the Trent Valley Malthouses, brewing being commonplace between here and Burton-on-Trent. The SSR junction was closed to passengers in January 1965, although it was retained for freight traffic for a few years longer. (*Author*)

BR Class 2–6–0 No. 78030 leaving Lichfield (Trent Valley) station on 22 August 1956 with the Crewe Signal and Telegraph Engineer's saloon M45010M. This saloon, shown here in early BR carmine and cream livery, was originally MR No. 2234, one of two steam railcars built in 1904. In 1917 the MR converted the vehicle for use as a business carriage and inspection saloon for the General Superintendent of the Line, Mr J.H. Follows. On 1 January 1946 twenty people were killed when a fish train ran into a stationary local train at Lichfield (Trent Valley) station. The accident, caused by frozen ballast which had jammed the points, was said at the time to have been unprecedented. (*P. Kendrick; F.W. Shuttleworth Collection*)

Ex-LMS Class 2P 4–4–0 No. 40692, having propelled the Walsall District Engineer's saloon No. M45044M through Lichfield (Trent Valley) station, now hauls it along the spur to the SSR line on 7 May 1959, in order to return to Walsall via Hammerwich and Pelsall. (*P. Kendrick; F.W. Shuttleworth Collection*)

Looking south just beyond Lichfield (Trent Valley) station a signalman/lampman is servicing signal gantry lamps in 1955. (*Roger Carpenter*)

Table 72	WALSALL, LICHFIELD AND BURTON-ON-TRENT TO DERBY			

A timetable for services between Lichfield (Trent Valley), Lichfield City (on the SSR), Walsall, Burton-on-Trent and Derby, during the summer of 1950. (Author's Collection)

42

Stanier 4–6–2 No. 46251 *City of Nottingham* heads the northbound 'Midday Scot' (identified by reporting No. W97) just north of Lichfield (Trent Valley) station on Saturday 26 June 1948. This is the first year of nationalization, and while the engine has been renumbered the tender retains the LMS sans-serif style of lettering introduced in 1946 and carried by relatively few engines. The train is approaching the original Trent Valley station; the present station was opened in 1871 at the point where the SSR Lichfield station between Birmingham and Derby crossed the Trent Valley Railway. The SSR also opened its own station at Lichfield at the same time. (*P. Kendrick; F.W. Shuttleworth Collection*)

Waiting at Tamworth (Low Level) station, with a Down express, is LNWR 'Jumbo' 2–4–0 No. 2194 *Cambrian, c.* 1920. (*Roger Carpenter Collection*)

Ex-LMS rebuilt 'Patriot' Class 4–6–0 No. 45523 *Bangor* is passing through Tamworth station, with an Up express for Euston, *c.* 1956. Tamworth was another of the 'First Class' stations opened with the TVR on 15 September 1847. As the MR's main Bristol–Derby line crossed the TVR at Tamworth, the station was also an important mail-exchange point until 1967 when mail trains were rerouted via Birmingham; all trains, with the exception of the 'Irish Mail' stopped here for exchange of mailbags between the TVR and the MR route. The MR actually arrived at Tamworth first when, as the Birmingham and Derby Junction Railway, its line arrived in the town on 12 August 1839. The TVR station at Tamworth had single-storey buildings, designed by John Livock, which were situated at the south end of the station on the Up platform. On the Down platform a two-storey building, in Jacobean style, was placed in the centre. The High and Low level stations are at right-angles to each other and were connected by lifts for mail exchange, and by a sharply curved spur for exchange of vehicles. The TVR runs at right-angles to, and passes underneath, the MR High Level station by means of a bridge. A chord line from the LNWR and MR was completed in June 1847. New Tamworth stations were opened on 24 September 1962, where efficient mail interchange facilities were major factors in their design, only for such facilities to cease some five years later. Just a few years after opening, the TVR was honoured with a Royal visit when, in 1853, Queen Victoria and Prince Albert traversed the line on their way from Osborne, on the Isle of Wight, to Balmoral, calling at Tamworth for lunch. The visit to Tamworth was, however, curtailed in an effort to make up time after a delayed sea-crossing from the Isle of Wight. Operation of the Royal Train over the TVR was a rare event, the Royal Family usually used the GWR line from Paddington to Wolverhampton gaining LNWR metals at Bushbury for the remainder of the journey to Scotland. (*Roger Carpenter*)

New Fowler designed LMS 'Royal-Scot' Class 4–6–0 No. 6163 *Civil Service Rifleman* heads the Down 'Irish Mail', from Euston to Holyhead, through Tamworth, 1931. Tamworth was the scene of an accident involving the 'Irish Mail' on 4 September 1870. There were two reasons why this accident occurred: lack of signal and points interlocking, which were only partial at Tamworth, and the fact that two signal cabins which controlled the line at this point were out of sight of each other because the overbridge carrying the MR's Bristol–Derby main line bisected Tamworth station. The station at this time had two platform roads that were loops off the fast lines and the points which controlled them were worked from the two signal-boxes. The 'Irish Mail' was some 13 minutes late as it approached Tamworth. The distant and outer home signals showed 'clear' as the train approached, so the driver kept the regulator open. The south-box signalman was expecting the 'Mail' and set his road accordingly, which meant that the Up platform road was open to the sidings. The north-box signalman was confused because his watch had stopped and he was expecting a goods train, so he had set his road for the Up platform. When he saw the light of the approaching 'Irish Mail' he thought it was a light engine. The 'Mail' ran over the crossover and through the Up platform road along the dead-end siding, then went through the stop block at the end of the siding, landing upright in the river. One passenger and the driver were killed, and the guard was seriously injured. The accident could have been avoided if the south-box signalman had realized his error and reset his points so that the train could regain the Up fast line. The inspector blamed a lack of communication for the accident, as well as obvious defects in signalling and points control. (*Author's Collection*)

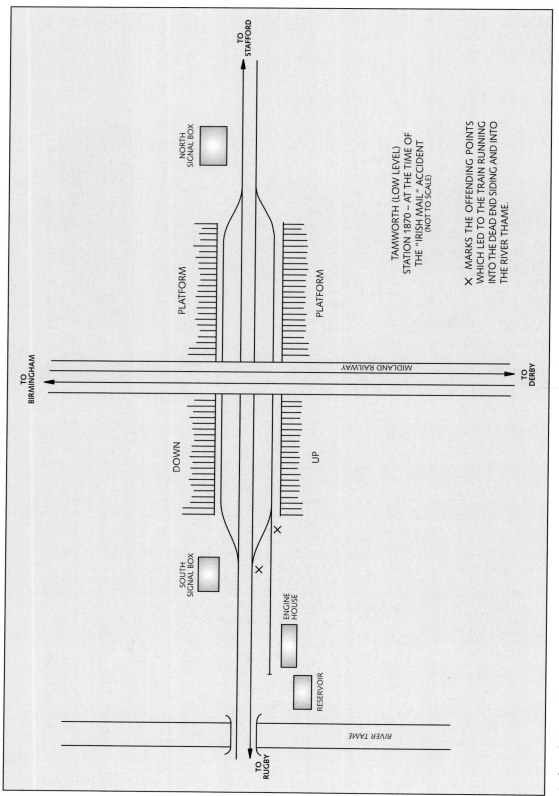

A plan of Tamworth station at the time of the 'Irish Mail' accident, showing the offending points which led to the train's misfortune. (*Author*)

Ex-LMS 'Princess-Coronation' Pacific No. 462400 *City of Coventry* hauls an Up express through Tamworth station in the late 1950s. Vandalism is seen as something of a modern problem, but this is not altogether true. In the first year of BR ownership, the railway suffered from this type of crime, and trainspotters were banned at many stations. One of the first stations where such a ban was introduced was at Tamworth in 1948, after track and installations had been damaged. (*Roger Carpenter*)

An unidentified LMS Class 5 4–6–0 heads an Up express under the bridge carrying the MR Bristol–Derby line over the TVR, 11 June 1935. Tamworth (High Level) station buildings can be seen above the train, along with the lift shafts for mail exchange between the stations. (*Roger Carpenter Collection*)

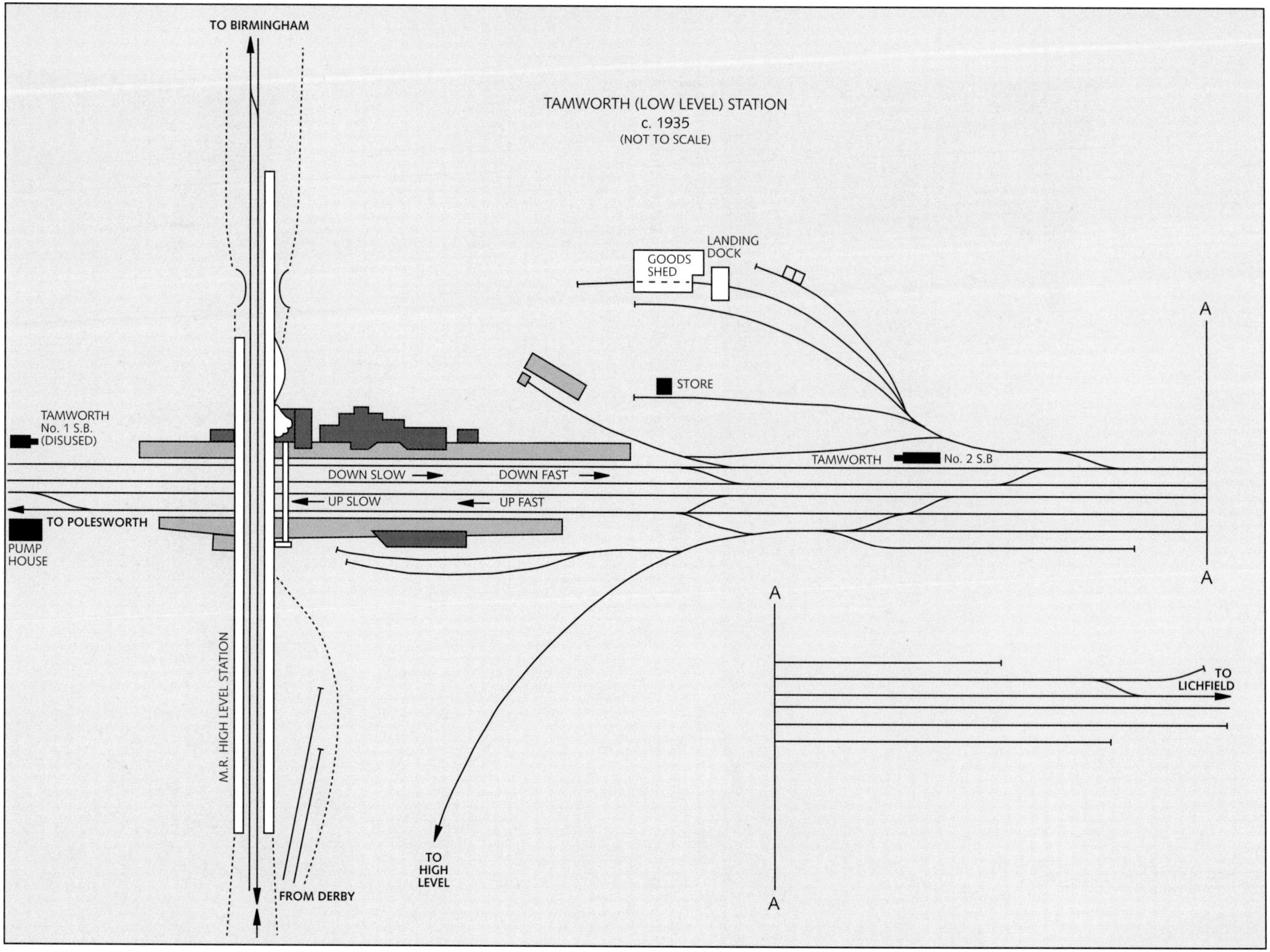

TAMWORTH (LOW LEVEL) STATION
c. 1935
(NOT TO SCALE)

TO LICHFIELD

A — A

No. 2 S.B

TAMWORTH

GOODS SHED

LANDING DOCK

STORE

TO HIGH LEVEL

DOWN FAST

UP FAST

DOWN SLOW

UP SLOW

FROM DERBY

M.R. HIGH LEVEL STATION

TO BIRMINGHAM

TAMWORTH No. 1 S.B. (DISUSED)

TO POLESWORTH

PUMP HOUSE

A plan of Tamworth (Low Level) station, along with the MR Derby–Bristol line and High Level station, *c.* 1935. (*Author*)

48

Approaching Tamworth (Low Level) is an express double headed by unrebuilt 'Patriot' Class 4–6–0 No. 45510 and rebuilt 'Royal-Scot' Class 4–6–0 No. 46100 *Royal Scot* herself, *c*, 1959. (*Roger Carpenter*)

Ex-LMS 'Princess-Coronation' Pacific No. 46256 *Sir William A. Stanier FRS* is passing Tamworth with a Down express for Glasgow, 1956. (*Roger Carpenter*)

Ex-LMS 2P 4–4–0 No. 40652 is leaving Tamworth (Low Level) station at the head of a local train for Stafford, mid-1950s. The train is passing one of the two signal-boxes which controlled the station while, in the background, the bridge carrying the Midland main line over the TVR can be seen. (*Roger Carpenter*)

Tamworth (High Level) station, 1988. This station replaced the original MR station when both it and the TVR station were rebuilt in 1962. (*Revd D. Hardy*)

CHAPTER THREE

LNWR STAFFORD

With the opening of the TVR Stafford became the second most important junction, after Crewe, on the LNWR. All trains between Scotland, the north-west of England and the North Wales coast (following the opening of the Chester and Holyhead Railway in 1848) to the West Midlands and London (Euston) passed through the station. Over the years all top-link LNWR, LMS and BR locomotives, hauled expresses through Stafford station. The TVR very quickly became Stafford's most important route, traffic on the GJR line to Birmingham dropping in volume.

Along with the opening of the TVR, the LNWR also took control of the Shropshire Union Canal and Railway Company, and its line from Stafford to Wellington was opened on 1 June 1849, after agreement had been reached with the SUC&R Co. in 1847. Originally the Shropshire company had planned to include a link between Crewe and Newtown, mid-Wales, and a route between Chester and Wolverhampton, which would have threatened the GJR. All of these plans were quietly forgotten once the Shropshire Union came under LNWR control, as no rival to the GJR would be tolerated. Opening of this branch gave the LNWR its own route between Wolverhampton and Shrewsbury, via Stafford, and started a war with the Shrewsbury and Birmingham Railway, who had dropped objections to the LNWR leasing the Shropshire Union route. The S&B line between Wolverhampton and Shewsbury was only 29¼ miles long, compared to the 46 miles of the Euston company's line. In an effort to destroy the S&B, the LNWR started a fare war, which involved both companies in expensive litigation, the Euston company being large enough to deal with the costs involved in both fare wars and litigation, in the hope that the S&B would go bankrupt. In the event, the S&B proved a strong company and even managed to reach agreement with the LNWR's enemy, the GWR, which brought unwanted competition to the Euston company for traffic to Merseyside, something Captain Huish had sought to avoid by trying to deny the Paddington company access to the Mersey ports.

Opening of the TVR and the branch to Wellington brought increased traffic to Stafford station, which was becoming inadequate for the new demands placed upon it. Matters were made more difficult with the introduction of local services between Stafford and Stoke-on-Trent, following consolidation of traffic arrangements between the LNWR and NSR, whose Acts of 13 August 1859 and 1866 allowed extensive running powers over each other's lines. Trains from Stafford to Stoke (and secondary services to Manchester via Macclesfield) gained NSR metals at Norton Bridge, which was opened to a temporary station at Stoke on 17 April 1848. Reciprocal running powers between the two companies brought the red locos and coaches of the NSR into Stafford, making an interesting contrast to the black locos and 'plum and spilt

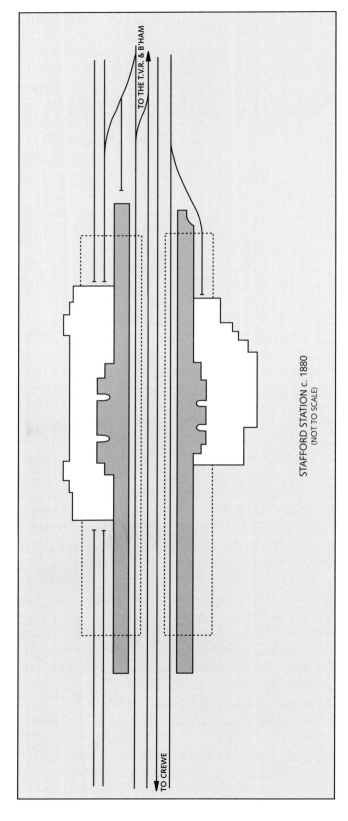

STAFFORD STATION c. 1880
(NOT TO SCALE)

TO THE T.V.R. & B'HAM

TO CREWE

A plan of the rebuilt Stafford station, *c.* 1880, having opened in 1861. In the early 1880s, further capacity was added when a through platform was built on the west side of the Down platform, converting it into an island, and numbered 3. (*Author*)

milk' carriages of the LNWR. Local services were also operated between Stafford and Walsall, via the TVR, to Rugeley and the South Staffordshire Railway via Cannock.

The original GJR Stafford station did not survive for long, being replaced by a new one in 1844. This new station had been designed by John Cunningham of Liverpool and was in Elizabethan style. Although it was intended to be permanent, it soon became clear that even this new structure was inadequate as it was small and badly laid out. When the LNWR decided, in 1860, to make Stafford the border between its northern and southern divisions this increased traffic demands at the station. In addition, traffic levels had expanded much more than had been anticipated and further expansion was being considered, meaning a new station had become a necessity.

Delays in the rebuilding of Stafford station may well have taken place because the 'Railway Mania' bubble had burst, and finance for major projects was much more difficult to obtain. Certainly, individual architectural styles for each station had become a thing of the past and a form of standardization was developed for station renewals across the country, giving a corporate image to the railway companies. The rebuilding of Stafford station fell into this new era, epitomized by the use of 'Euston'-style iron and glass roofs over the platforms. This new Stafford station, designed by LNWR architect, W. Baker, was situated a little distance north of the previous one and opened in 1861.

Exterior of the 1861-built Stafford station with the North Western Hotel on the right. John Parnell of Rugby was awarded the contract to build the new station, and was provided with two long platforms on each side of the four track formation which passed through the station. Each platform face was served by a single platform line, and two through roads ran through the middle of the station. The station buildings incorporated several architectural styles, thanks to previous work done by the GJR. The station exterior, on the east side, was provided with a large canopy to the grand entrance which had twin classical columns supporting a semi-circular arched window surround in one part and plain segmented arches in another. Access to the platforms was via a footbridge, which was basically a large steel box girder with wood panelling, partially glazed and braced at the roof with cast-iron members. The station was also provided with goods lines, on the west side, which ran behind the Down platform and gave access to the locoshed. (*F.W. Shuttleworth Collection*)

The main Up platform 1, with station staff, *c.* 1900. The crowd behind have come from the train in the GNR bay at the far end of the platform. A Down train is at platform 2 and a light engine is on the Down through line. This Up platform was 740 ft long, while the Down platform was 720 ft long. Each platform had bays at both ends. The bay at the south end of the Up platform was for local trains operating over the TVR, while those at the north were for Crewe-bound locals. The bay at the south end of the Down platform were for Birmingham locals; those at the north end were used by locals for Stoke-on-Trent. When GNR services started in 1881 they used the northern bay of the Up platform. The whole station was covered by two 'Euston'-style roofs of wrought iron and glass, some 530 ft long, over the two sides of the station, leaving the two fast lines in the centre uncovered. The pitched roofs were supported on cast-iron columns in the centre, forming an arcade, and on brick walls behind the bay tracks. Ornate ironwork was used on the valances above the platforms. (*F.W. Shuttleworth Collection*)

'Lady of the Lake' Class 2–2–2, No. 818 *Havelock* is acting as pilot on a Down express at Stafford, *c.* 1904. Many of these simple and robust engines were shedded at Stafford for use on 'Irish Mail' services between Euston and Holyhead. As Stafford was the boundary between northern and southern divisions of the LNWR locomotives were changed here until transfer to Crewe. (*Roger Carpenter Collection*)

At the head of an Up express, LNWR Webb 'Dreadnought' 2–2–2–0 compound loco No. 510 *Leviathan* waits on Platform 1, 1904. In the 1880s, Anglo-Scottish expresses made a stop at Stafford where passengers could obtain luncheon baskets. For 3s, these baskets contained half a chicken with ham or tongue or a portion of cold beef, salad, ice, bread, cheese, butter, etc., with either half a bottle of claret, two glasses of sherry or a pint bottle of stout. (*Roger Carpenter Collection*)

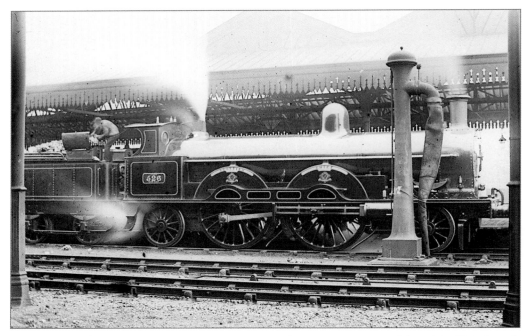

Waiting at Stafford station is LNWR 'Greater Britain' 2–2–2–2 compound loco No. 526 *Scottish Chief, c.* 1904. The driver appears to be busying himself in the toolbox on the tender. The Euston-style roof above the platform can be clearly seen here. (*Roger Carpenter Collection*)

Double heading an unidentified loco, LNWR 'Dreadnought' 2–2–2–0 compound loco No. 508 *Titan* is standing on the Birmingham end of the island platform at Stafford station, 1904. (*Roger Carpenter Collection*)

Taking on water at the south end of Stafford station is 'Precedent' Class 2–4–0 (also known as 'Jumbos') No. 260 *Duke of Connaught, c.* 1904. (*Roger Carpenter Collection*)

Another 'Precedent' or 'Jumbo' 2–4–0 No. 1683 *Sisyphus* is viewed from platform 1, while the engine is on platform 3 with a train for Birmingham. The photograph gives a good view of the station roof and its columns. (*Roger Carpenter Collection*)

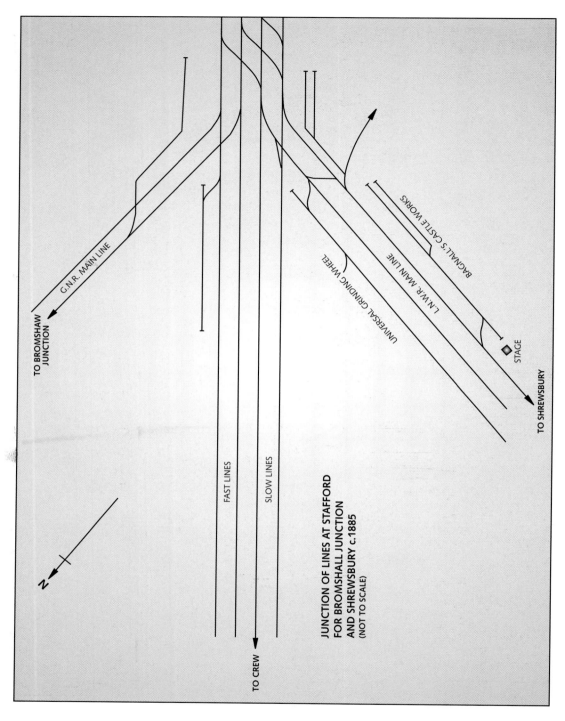

Northern junctions at Stafford showing the main line to Crewe, and the branch to Shrewsbury (on the left), with sidings to Bagnall's locoworks and Universal Grinding Wheel Company. *c.* 1885. On the right is the GNR line to Bromshall Junction. (*Author*)

Double heading with another loco at Stafford is LNWR 4–4–0 loco No. 1973 *Hood* with a Down express on No. 2 Platform, 1904. (*Roger Carpenter Collection*)

At the head of an Up express for Euston is LNWR 'Dreadnought' 2–2–2–0 compound No. 659 at platform 1, Stafford, 1904. (*Roger Carpenter Collection*)

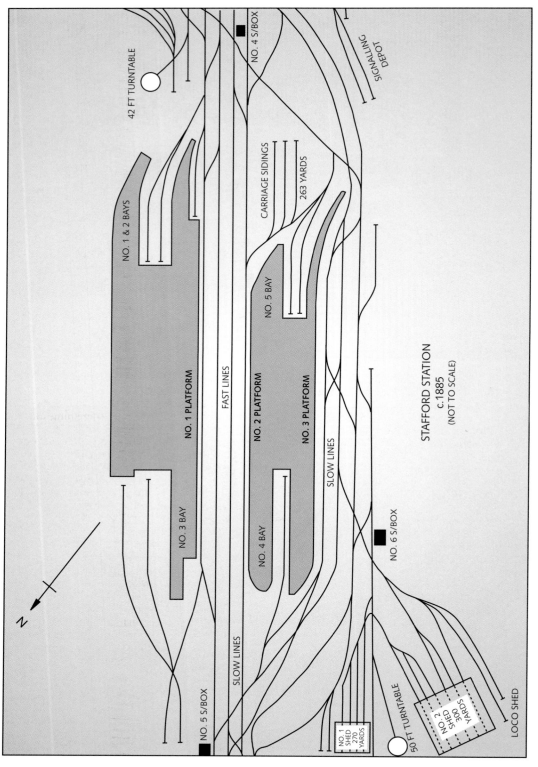

A plan of Stafford station, *c.* 1885. The island platform is now in use. At first this new No. 3 platform was used for Up trains, but in 1883 the Board of Trade agreed to the use of a scissors crossing in the centre of the platform, the first such crossing ever used in Britain, enabling platform 3 to be used by trains from either direction. To the south of the station the tracks of the TVR and GJR merged, as both trains from Euston and Birmingham had to use the same track formation through the station and delays were often caused by conflicting movements. (*Author*)

Within the plan:

42 FT TURNTABLE

NO. 4 S/BOX

SIGNALLING DEPOT

NO. 1 & 2 BAYS

CARRIAGE SIDINGS

263 YARDS

NO. 5 BAY

NO. 1 PLATFORM

FAST LINES

NO. 2 PLATFORM

NO. 3 PLATFORM

NO. 3 BAY

NO. 4 BAY

SLOW LINES

NO. 6 S/BOX

STAFFORD STATION
c.1885
(NOT TO SCALE)

N

SLOW LINES

NO. 5 S/BOX

NO. 1 SHED 270 YARDS

NO. 2 SHED 300 YARDS

50 FT TURNTABLE

LOCO SHED

Wellington station, terminus of the LNWR branch from Stafford and on the GWR main line from Wolverhampton to Shrewsbury, with examples of LMS and GWR tank engines in view, in the 1930s. Wellington was the focus of a dispute with Captain Mark Huish, General Manager of the LNWR, and the little S&B, Huish doing his best to put the S&B out of business, using the muscle of the much larger LNWR to destroy any competition. In the end, the S&B joined forces with the GWR to give the Paddington company a route to the Mersey, something that the LNWR had sought to prevent over the years as it tried to maintain a monopoly of Liverpool traffic. The LNWR had been in dispute with the S&B over the Shrewsbury company's plans to operate trains from Shrewsbury to Birmingham (New Street), via the LNWR-owned Stour Valley line from Wolverhampton since 1850, which had led to violence and litigation, and further trouble ensued over respective routes between Wolverhampton and Wellington. The LNWR leased the Shropshire Union Railways and Canal Company and opened its line from Stafford to Wellington on 1 June 1849, in its bid to thwart GWR ambitions of reaching Merseyside. Huish had obtained an agreement with the S&B to take control of the Shropshire Union route but, in contravention of this agreement, began a fare war with the S&B between Wolverhampton and Wellington. The S&B's 29½-mile line was shorter than that of the LNWR, whose line ran from Wolverhampton, down the GJR to Stafford and thence along the Shropshire Union line, and was 46 miles long. The loss of a few thousand pounds meant little to Huish if it meant that he could destroy the S&B. His pretext was that the LNWR had no legal powers to make any agreements and matters went to litigation. While all of these disputes were going on, except in 1850 when an injunction was in force, passengers were carried between Wolverhampton and Shrewsbury at very low fares, eventually fixed at First Class 1s, Second Class 9d, Third Class 6d. As a comparison, fares between Wellington and Shrewsbury, over the joint line, were 6d, 3d and 1d respectively. While these disputes raged on, the LNWR developed the Stafford–Wellington line, especially the approach to Wellington where industry and mining were fast developing and a fairly intensive service was operated. By July 1914, there were fourteen trains each way per day between Stafford, Wellington and Shrewsbury. As an ironic footnote, the LNWR line to Wellington has gone, while the GWR/S&B line is still open. (*Author's Collection*)

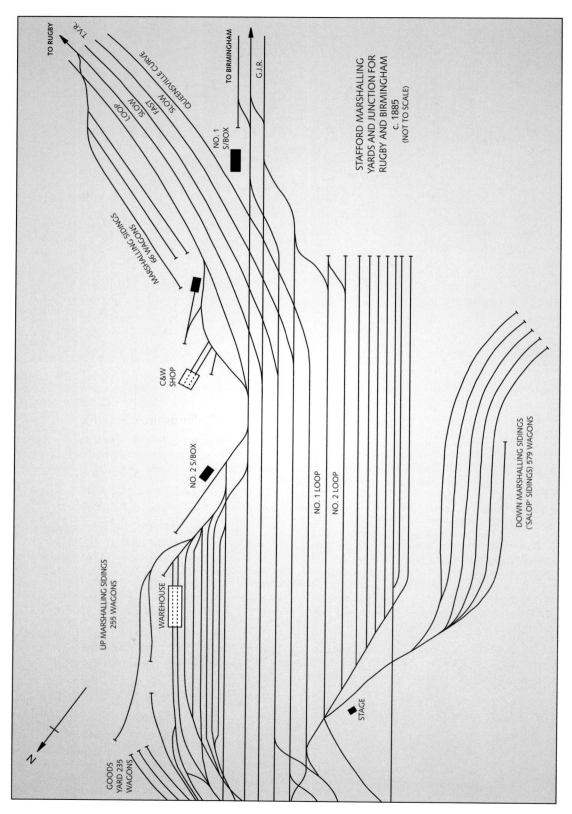

A plan of tracks south of Stafford station, *c.* 1885, showing the junction of lines for Rugby (the TVR) and for Birmingham (the GJR), as well as the complex of goods yards. (*Author*)

CHAPTER FOUR

THE GREAT NORTHERN RAILWAY AT STAFFORD

Stafford was the furthest west reached by the GNR over its own metals with its single line which left the LNWR main line just north of the station to Bromshall Junction, near Uttoxeter, where it joined the NSR's Crewe–Derby line. The GNR had running powers over the NSR as far as Eggington Junction, for access to Derby Friargate station, where connections could be made for Nottingham and Grantham.

Although Stafford was the most westerly outpost of King's Cross, the GNR's intention had been to reach Wales, following its successful penetration into the Nottinghamshire coalfield and the Stafford and Uttoxeter Railway, incorporated on 29 July 1862 and opened on 23 December 1867, was to be the instrument by which the GNR could reach its goal. The S&UR had received little opposition when its Bill was presented to Parliament but, at committee stage, a clause was inserted to reduce its powers by preventing the GNR using running powers over NSR metals, at the insistence of LNWR directors who were concerned that the new line would 'divert traffic' by any circuitous route from lines of the LNWR or Staffordshire companies.

On incorporation, the S&UR, whose registered office was in Wellington, was given five years to build its 13¼-mile line and a 2-mile branch to Weston on the NSR between Stone and Colwich. The line, however, was in financial difficulties from its earliest days owing to the clauses inserted in its final Act, combined with lack of revenue because of small passenger numbers as the line passed through rural Staffordshire. Its situation only improved when the GNR took an interest in the line.

The GNR became interested in the S&UR following further expansion beyond Staffordshire and into Derbyshire, the company completing and opening a line from Colwick to Pinxton in 1875 and from Ashworth Junction to Eggington three years later. This latter line was mainly to serve Burton-on-Trent. In order to strike further west in an effort to reach Wales, the King's Cross company bought the S&UR for £100,000 in July 1881, operating a service to Stafford the same year. The NSR welcomed the GNR because it believed that the LNWR line to Euston might not be the only one to London, despite the friendly relations that existed between the NSR and LNWR.

Despite its isolation from the main system the S&UR had a distinctive GNR character and the King's Cross company even had its own goods facilities at Stafford Doxey Road, being reached by a ¼-mile long branch. The GNR also maintained a stationmaster and staff of eleven at Stafford's LNWR station until 1915, when the LNWR took over these duties. Stafford Common station, too, had its own stationmaster.

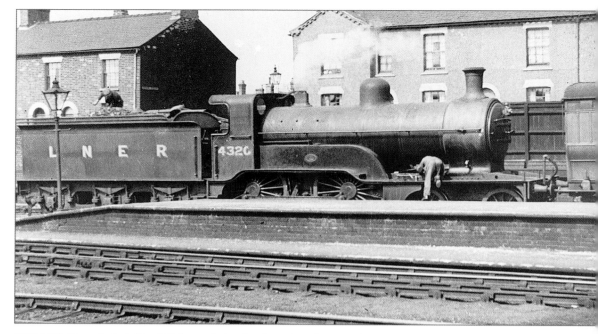

LNER D2 Class 4–4–0 No. 4320 stands in the Great Northern Railway (GNR) bay in 1938, having arrived from Derby at 3.32 p.m., run round its train and pushed it back into the platform. It will go to Stafford locoshed to turn before taking the 4.37 p.m. train back to Derby. (*P. Kendrick; F.W. Shuttleworth Collection*)

The GNR passed to LNER ownership following the 1923 'Grouping' and ex-GNR 0–6–0 and 4–4–0 tender engines operated passenger services until these trains ceased operating on 4 December 1939, after the outbreak of the Second World War, never to return. Freight traffic was usually handled by small 0–6–0 tender engines. The line survived for a further twelve years, despite loss of passenger services, to serve an RAF camp which had been established near Stafford Common station, special servicemen's trains running into the station. The line between Stafford Common (Air Ministry Sidings) and Bromshall Junction was finally closed to all traffic on 5 March 1951.

The north end of Stafford station, looking from Bagnall's locoworks bridge, 1938. On the left is LNER Class J6 0–6–0 No. 3623, leaving the GNR bay with a local train to Uttoxeter. An Up goods train is standing on the fast line, while an LMS 4F 0–6–0 is on the section between the platform line and the Down slow line. An ex-NSR tank loco is standing bunker first in No. 4 bay, probably having just been released after arriving with a local train from the Potteries, by another loco removing its train, and is now awaiting a clear road to the locoshed. The LNER train will soon take the right-hand branch for Stafford Common and Bromshall Junction, to gain access to Uttoxeter. (*P. Kendrick; F.W. Shuttleworth Collection*)

LNER 4–4–0 No. 4363 near Hopton, on the outskirts of Stafford, with a train from Derby and Uttoxeter, *c.* 1930. The Second World War RAF base was established close to here and allowed the branch to survive beyond 1939 after regular passenger service ceased. (*P. Kendrick; F.W. Shuttleworth Collection*)

LNER 4–4–0 No. 4329 at Bromshall Junction with a train for Stafford, *c.* 1930. Trains from Uttoxeter had to stop here to take the tablet for single line working. Here, the driver is climbing down from his engine to collect the tablet from the signal-box. (*P. Kendrick; F.W. Shuttleworth Collection*)

LNER 4–4–0 No. 4353 leaves the tunnel near Bromshall Junction with a train from Stafford, *c.* 1930. (*P. Kendrick; F.W. Shuttleworth Collection*)

On 23 March 1957 the Stephenson's Locomotive Society ran the Uttoxeter GNR Tour from Stafford and over the old GNR route to Uttoxeter via Bromshall Junction, this being the last train over the line. Here, at Stafford, the special hauled by ex-LMS Ivatt 2–6–2 tank loco, still sporting early BR livery, No. 41224, is waiting to depart from Stafford station with the special train. (*H.F. Wheeller Collection/Roger Carpenter*)

The SLS special is leaving Stafford, 23 March 1957. (*H.F. Wheeller Collection/Roger Carpenter*)

The SLS special is seen here leaving the LNWR main line and entering the ex-GNR branch, as it heads towards Stafford Common station. (*H.F. Wheeller Collection/Roger Carpenter*)

Leaving Stafford, the SLS special makes its way towards Stafford Common station. (*H.F. Wheeller Collection/ Roger Carpenter*)

The SLS special enters the single line GNR branch to Bromshall Junction and passes the Venables Ground Frame, which controls the entry point to the branch. (*H.F. Wheeller Collection/Roger Carpenter*)

The SLS special approaches the road overbridge as it heads towards Stafford Common station. The old booking office can be seen above on the bridge. (*H.F. Wheeller Collection/ Roger Carpenter*)

The SLS special passes the former waiting room at Stafford Common station. (*H.F. Wheeller Collection/ Roger Carpenter*)

Ingestre and Weston station, GNR, looking towards Stafford from the signal-box on 26 December 1954. (*P. Kendrick; F.W. Shuttleworth Collection*)

The signal-box and the platform for Stafford trains, Ingestre and Weston, 26 December 1954. (*P. Kendrick; F.W. Shuttleworth Collection*)

The main station buildings and the platform for Uttoxeter trains, at Ingestre and Weston, GNR, on 26 December 1954. (*P. Kendrick; F.W. Shuttleworth Collection*)

Grindley station was set in pleasant rural surroundings. The platforms here were staggered; this view, taken from the signal-box, shows the main station buildings and the platform for Uttoxeter trains, 26 December 1954. The track east of Stafford Common was lifted in 1959, but the section between Stafford Common and the west coast main line was retained for use by engineers during electrification; this stub was taken out of use in December 1975. (*P. Kendrick; F.W. Shuttleworth Collection*)

CHAPTER FIVE

THE POST-GROUPING YEARS

Immediately after the 'Grouping', which transferred Stafford from the LNWR to the LMSR from 1 January 1923, there was very little change as LNWR motive power was still very much the order of the day, but this only increased the intense rivalry between the two most important of the old companies which formed part of the new LMS. These were the MR, with its headquarters at Derby, and the LNWR locomotive headquarters at Crewe. Rivalry continued for the best part if a decade although it was MR influence that won the day, until the appointment of W.A. Stanier, from the GWR, in 1932. Appointment of Sir Henry Fowler, who had been CME at Derby, to the same post on the LMS in 1925 brought an influx of ex-MR loco types on trains at Stafford, as Fowler chose to continue with MR designs for the LMS. This, in essence, meant three-cylinder 'Compound' 4–4–0s for express work, 2P 4–4–0s for secondary duties, along with 3F and 4F 0–6–0s for freight, and 3F 0–6–0 tanks for shunting work. Unfortunately, these small engines were to prove unsatisfactory on the Euston–Glasgow expresses, many of these prestigious trains having to be double-headed, and journey times were slower than they had been prior to the First World War.

Such was the inadequacy of these small MR engines that the LMS arranged the loan of GWR 'Castle' Class 4–6–0 No. 5000 *Launceston Castle* for trial on Euston–Glasgow expresses and Stafford was to see the engine pass through on such services for several weeks. The GWR loco proved to be the master of any schedule given to it and the LMS were so impressed that they asked the GWR to build some 'Castle' Class engines for them, but the Paddington company refused and Fowler was asked to design 4–6–0s of his own. These turned out to be the famous 'Royal Scot' Class and they were first put on the Glasgow services, until replaced by Stanier's famous 'Princess' and 'Duchess' Pacifics. From 1930, the 'Royal Scot' locos were more associated with 'Irish Mail' trains which ran between Euston and Holyhead, via Stafford.

Competition between the LMS and LNER over Scottish services became very fierce by the mid-1930s, with the LNER's Sir Nigel Gresley introducing his famous streamlined A4 Pacifics in 1935 on the 'Silver Jubilee' express, to be followed a year later by the non-stop 'Coronation' train. On the LMS a non-stop train was run from Euston to Glasgow, using Pacific No. 6201 *Princess Elizabeth* on 16 November 1936, which created a record for the longest non-stop run for the engine. In 1937, the LMS introduced its own streamlined engines, the famous 'Duchess' Pacific, on Scottish expresses. The first of these locos, No. 6220 *Coronation*, emerged from Crewe

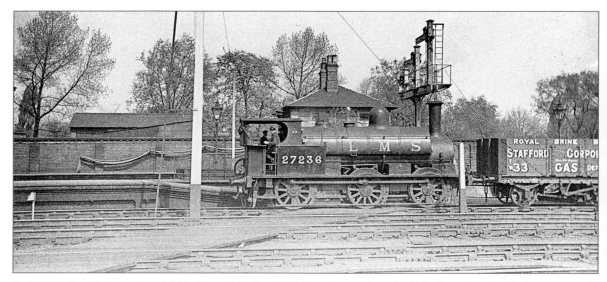

Ex-LNWR Ramsbottom 'Special Tank' as LMS No. 27236, at the south end of Platform 1 at Stafford station, mid-1930s. The loco is propelling wagons into the sidings south of Newport Road bridge, the 'calling-on' signal on the gantry above the engine is 'off'; the other two signals control the exit from the platform to the Up slow line and to the Up fast line. The wagon of Stafford Corporation Gas Department is believed to have been painted bright red. Above the loco is the roof of the stationmaster's house. During electrification, the stationmaster was rehoused and his old house was used as the BR Staff Association club, after the station was demolished and until a new one was built near the coal wharf. (*P. Kendrick; F.W. Shuttleworth Collection*)

in that year and were to become a common sight at Stafford on top-link expresses. In connection with these high-speed services, the Trent Valley Junction at Stafford was realigned in the summer of 1938. The TVR approached the original GJR line from Birmingham by the 25-chain Queensville Curve, which imposed a 30 mph speed restriction for nearly ¾-mile. To raise the permitted speed to 55 mph, the junctions were relaid with two level chairs and switch diamonds were installed. The less important GJR route was realigned, with permitted speed remaining at 30 mph. Queensville Curve was slewed by up to 11 ft 7 in and given an additional cant. The scheme cost £8,000 for track and £2,000 for track alterations.

Outbreak of the Second World War put an end to LMS and LNER rivalry, and the 'Duchesses' were de-streamlined during the war. The post-war period saw the railways nationalized from 1 January 1948. While still in LMS ownership, Stafford station was affected by severe flooding in February 1946, after heavy rain caused the River Sow to burst its banks, and the station was closed for two or three days as water covered the railway tracks up to a level with the platform edges.

Viewed from 'Bagnall's Bridge', an unidentified ex-LNWR 'Claughton' Class 4–6–0 hauls a thirteen-coach express from Crewe into Stafford station, 1934. Signals on the gantry above the train have rings below the Home semaphores controlling the slow lines. This was standard practice in LNWR days, but the LMS later removed them. On the right is the junction for the GNR line to Bromshall Junction, with a GNR concrete signal post at the mouth, just in front of Venables timber yard (the yard is still in existence today). On the left is the old LNWR branch to Wellington. In LMS days, 'The Welshman' express, which ran between Euston and the North Wales seaside resorts, had a coach attached for Swansea which was detached at Stafford. It was then attached to a train which ran down the branch to Wellington, later being put on a train which ran along the Central Wales line to reach Swansea, a very roundabout route indeed. It was during the 1920s that many express trains were given names by the Commercial Department of the LMS as there were problems with motive power used on many of the company's express trains, and trains were slow by comparison with others of the 'Big Four'. Titles were invented in 1927, including 'The Royal Scot', and the new LMS 4–6–0, designed following trials with GWR 'Castle' Class 4–6–0 No. 5000, *Launceston Castle*, No. 6100, was named after the train as this Class was intended for use on Scottish expresses. (*P. Kendrick; F.W. Shuttleworth Collection*)

The north end of Platform 2 at Stafford station, 27 January 1935. 'The Royal Scot' is approaching on the Up fast line, headed by LMS 'Princess Royal' Pacific No. 6200 *The Princess Royal*, doyen of a class of twelve engines, built by W.A. Stanier for Scottish expresses. No. 6200 emerged from Crewe works in 1933 and sister engine No. 6201 *Princess Elizabeth* (now preserved) held the record for the longest non-stop run (from Euston to Glasgow in 1936), as competition with the LNER's East Coast route for Scottish services intensified, resulting in the development of the streamlined 'Princess Coronation' Pacifics for Scottish expresses in 1937. Once the new streamlined Pacifics had come into service, the 'Princess Royal' Pacifics spent most of their working lives on Euston–Liverpool expresses, many being shedded at Liverpool (Edge Hill). Streamlining on the 'Princess Coronation' Pacifics was removed between 1946 and 1949. One other member of the 'Princess Royal' Class, No. 6202, was built as a *Turbomotive* engine and put into service on Liverpool expresses in 1935. It was rebuilt as a conventional loco in 1952 and named *Princess Anne*, but was destroyed in the Harrow accident in October of that year. In this view, No. 6200 is in original condition, with small tender and LNWR shed plate No. 1 (Camden) on the smokebox door. On the left in this view, an Up goods train passes the locoshed on the extreme left on the slow line hauled by ex-LNWR 'Super D' 0–8–0, while further left is an ex-NSR tank loco standing behind the shed. The signal on the gantry in the foreground is 'off' for the Down fast line. Other signals on the gantry are for diversions from the Down fast, from left to right, to the Wellington branch, the Down slow, and the GNR line. (*P. Kendrick; F.W. Shuttleworth Collection*)

LMS Stanier 5XP 'Jubilee' Class 4–6–0 No. 5553, later to be named *Canada*, stands at the south end of Stafford station with an Up express, *c.* 1934. (*P. Kendrick; F.W. Shuttleworth Collection*)

LMS 6P 'Royal Scot' Class 4–6–0 No. 6137 *Vesta* heads an Up express at the south end of Stafford station, 1934. The loco was not to retain its original name, being renamed *The Prince of Wales's Volunteers South Lancashire* when it was decided to name all but No. 6100 after British military regiments. (*P. Kendrick; F.W. Shuttleworth Collection*)

A view of Stafford station looking south, showing the station buildings and complex of tracks at the north end of the station, *c.* 1934. Hughes-Fowler 'Crab', Class 5, 2–6–0 No. 13238 is at the head of a Down fitted freight. (*P. Kendrick; F.W. Shuttleworth Collection*)

Ex-LNWR Ramsbottom 0–6–0 'Special Tank', as LMS No. 27236, shunts vans in the bay at the south end of Stafford station Down platform, 1935. Only four years later, Britain was again at war with Germany, and when it was over the railways were in a dilapidated state, and there were calls for nationalization. A new Labour government, elected in 1945, was keen to bring key industries under State control and the railways were nationalized in 1948. (*P. Kendrick; F.W. Shuttleworth Collection*)

CHAPTER SIX

STAFFORD LOCOSHED

Stafford was a stabling point for locomotives from the opening of the GJR line, although no shed building existed until the 1850s when the LNWR had control of the line. Francis Trevithick, who was locomotive superintendent for the Northern Division at Crewe, made several requests for covered accommodation but the LNWR committee did not give approval until 1852, with a shed holding twelve engines being built soon afterwards.

As a junction of the TVR and the GJR line between Birmingham and Liverpool, the LNWR decided, in 1860, to make Stafford the limit of both Northern and Southern Divisions and to build 'an independent Engine Shed' for the Southern Division at Stafford. The existing Northern Division shed was to be extended. In April of that year a Mr Parnall, who had built a number of locosheds for the LNWR, won the contract for this work, at a cost of £2,750 10s. The new Southern Division shed opened the following year, it being a brick-built structure with hipped roof. The new shed had six roads, and was later designated 'No. 2' shed. The older four-road structure, which stood nearer to the main line, was designated 'No. 1' shed. Both buildings had offices and stores to the rear, those of the older building being surmounted by a water tank. A 45-ft turntable, later enlarged to 50 ft, was placed between them, and in August 1866 track in the yard was rearranged to ease engine movements between the two sheds. John Ramsbottom, LNWR locomotive superintendent, had reported to the committee that 'great inconvenience is experienced for want of a crossover road from one steam shed to the other'. It was recommended 'that one be put down immediately, at a cost estimated by Mr Woodhouse of £66'.

From this point, until the turn of the century, Stafford shed was at the height of its importance, handling many express passenger locos from both the Northern and Southern Divisions. As Stafford was the limit of both Divisions, express engines were changed here. As the nineteenth century drew to a close many of these loco changes were undertaken at Crewe, and Stafford shed began to decline from its former importance. By the 'Grouping' its allocation had been reduced to only forty engines. Stafford had no sub-sheds and was coded 14 by the LNWR, becoming 5C under LMS auspices in 1935. At this time the shed had lost most of its former importance and its loco allocation was more than halved. Such was its decline that Stafford shed had a surplus of space – a very unusual situation at that time.

Under LMS control some improvements were undertaken. The turntable was enlarged to 60 ft in 1937/8, although the railway company had considered installing a 70-ft unit. The original 'No. 1' shed was in a dilapidated condition by this time and was demolished, leaving only the rear offices, stores and water tank.

Ex-LNWR 'Precursor' Class 4–4–0 No. 5279 *Sunbeam* at Stafford shed, April 1933. Although Stafford had come under LMS control by this time, the shed still had an allocation of ex-LNWR engines, giving an idea of the types of locos that were allocated to the shed in pre-grouping days. (*Author's Collection*)

A coaling plant and ash disposal apparatus, manufactured by Henry Lees & Co., were installed at the shed in the mid-1930s and the roof of 'No. 2' shed was renewed in 1947.

In the early 1950s, following nationalization, Stafford shed had an allocation of some twenty-four locos and these reflected the nature of traffic for which the shed provided motive power. For heavy freight there were around six ex-LNWR 0–8–0 tender engines, replaced by ex-LMS Class 5 4–6–0s and 8F 2–8–0s in the early 1960s. A few class 3F 0–6–0s were allocated for shunting and local goods work, and ex-LMS 2–6–4 tanks were shedded at Stafford to handle local passenger trains. After a long decline, Stafford shed was closed on 19 July 1965.

Ex-LNWR 18-in goods loco, known as 'Cauliflowers', No. 8525 (LNWR No. 121) at Stafford shed, 1934. As the limit of both Northern and Southern divisions, the shed was at the height of its importance until the turn of the nineteenth century and it handled many express passenger locomotives from both the Northern and Southern Divisions. In the very early days, the shed would have handled the brick-red liveried engines of the Southern Division and the blackberry-black of the Northern Division, until John Ramsbottom became CME for the LNWR, and took all locomotive affairs to Crewe, with all of the company's engines being turned out in blackberry-black from 1862. As Stafford was the limit of both Divisions, express engines were changed here. As the nineteenth century drew to a close many loco changes were undertaken at Crewe, and Stafford shed declined in importance. (*Author's Collection*)

Ex-LNWR 'Special Tank' No. 7236 (LNWR No. 3613) at Stafford shed, April 1933. These engines were allocated to Stafford shed for use on shunting duties and local freight work. (*Author's Collection*)

A pair of ex-LMS Fowler 2–6–4 tank engines, Nos 42350 and 42381, at the side of Stafford shed, 26 March 1965. (*P. Kendrick; F.W. Shuttleworth Collection*)

Viewed from the Newport Road bridge, ex-LNWR 0–8–0 No. 49079 and ex-LMS 8F 2–8–0 No. 48762, coupled light engine, approach Stafford from the south, 18 March 1962. The Stanier 2–8–0 was built at Doncaster in January 1946 as LNER No. 3157, and was renumbered 3557 in March 1947. It was transferred to the LMS in October 1947 and renumbered 8762, becoming BR No. 48762 in November 1948, and was withdrawn from service in February 1966. Originally the engine was paired with a Stanier curved top tender, but towards the end of its working life it ran coupled to a straight sided tender. (*P. Kendrick; F.W. Shuttleworth Collection*)

0–8–0 No. 49079 and 2–8–0 No. 48762, having worked in from the south coupled light engine, reverse past Stafford No. 5 signal-box on to the shed lines, 18 March 1962. (*P. Kendrick: F.W. Shuttleworth Collection*)

Ex-MR 3F 0–6–0 No. 43948 at Stafford shed, 1950. (*Roger Carpenter Collection*)

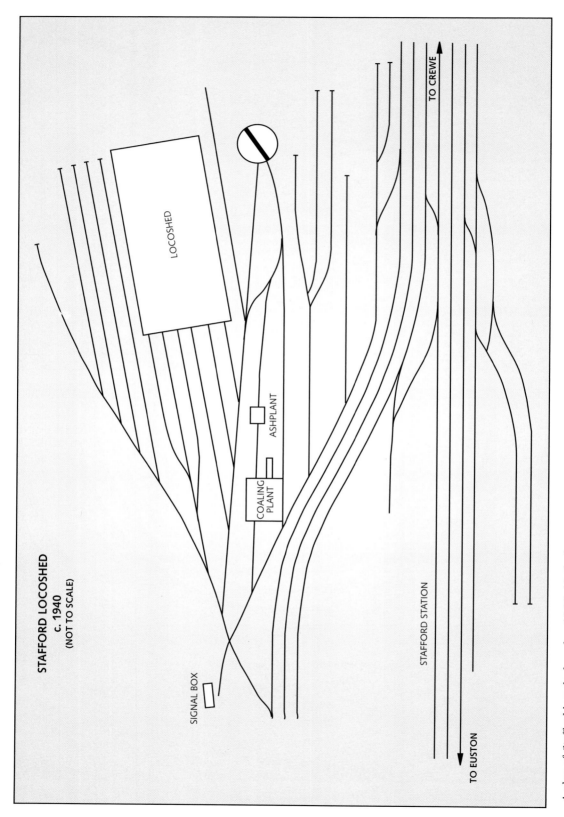

STAFFORD LOCOSHED
c. 1940
(NOT TO SCALE)

LOCOSHED

ASHPLANT

COALING PLANT

SIGNAL BOX

STAFFORD STATION

TO CREWE

TO EUSTON

A plan of Stafford locoshed yard, c. 1940. (*Author*)

Stafford locoshed, showing some of its allocation of 2–6–4 tank locos and ex-LMS Stanier 8F heavy freight engines, 22 April 1962. In the background, on the left, is a sign that steam traction's days are numbered, as a Modernization Plan Diesel Multiple Unit two car set is parked. These units would take over the role of the 2–6–4 tank engine as the mainstay of local train services. By the early 1950s, following nationalization, Stafford shed had an allocation of around twenty-four engines, these reflecting the nature of the traffic for which the shed provided motive power. For heavy freight work there were around half a dozen ex-LNWR 0–8–0 tender engines, which were replaced by ex-LMS Class Five 4–6–0s and 8F 2–8–0s in the early 1960s. There were also six Class 3F 0–6–0 tanks for shunting and local goods work, replacing the ex-LNWR 'Special Tanks', and ex-LMS Fowler 2–6–4 tanks to handle local passenger trains to Wolverhampton and Shrewsbury. By the early 1960s, most of these Fowler tanks were replaced by Stanier types. The remainder of the allocation was made up of ex-Midland Railway and LMS 2P 4–4–0s which had all gone by 1960. (*Roger Carpenter*)

Ex-LMS Fowler 2–6–4 tank loco No. 42389 is seen near the coaling stage at Stafford shed, late 1950s. These engines were the mainstay of motive power for local passenger trains until replaced by modern Diesel Multiple Unit trains as part of the 1955 'Modernization Plan'. (*Roger Carpenter*)

Ex-LMS Fowler 3F 0–6–0T No. 47665 in steam at Stafford shed on 26 March 1965. This engine had been allocated to Stafford for at least fifteen years; at one time, when the yards were busy with loose-coupled goods trains, Stafford shed never had less than six of these engines which were employed on shunting duties, and on transfer work between the Stafford goods yards. (*P. Kendrick; F.W. Shuttleworth Collection*)

Opposite: Stafford shed, on Friday 26 March 1965, four months before closure. Fowler 0–6–0T No. 47665 (in steam) is at the side of the shed, while in front of the building are ex-LMS Stanier 2–8–0 No. 48340 (fitted with straight sided tender) and Class 5 4–6–0 No. 44714. (*P. Kendrick; F.W. Shuttleworth Collection*)

Stanier Class 8F 2–8–0 No. 48340, fitted with straight-sided tender, at Stafford shed on Friday 26 March 1965. There were just six other engines on shed at this time: two Fowler 2–6–4T engines, Nos 42350 and 42381 (in store at the side of the shed), Fowler 0–6–0T No. 47665, and Stanier Class 5 4–6–0 mixed traffic engines Nos 44714, 45048 and 45374. (P. Kendrick; F.W. Shuttleworth Collection)

Stafford Shed Allocations

4 November 1950

MR 2P 4–4–0	40322, 40405, 40443, 40461, 40471, 40507
LMS Fowler 2–6–4T	42309, 42320, 42345, 42346, 42347, 42391
LMS 3F 0–6–0T	47588, 47598, 47606, 47649, 47653, 47665
LNWR 0–8–0	48922, 49047, 49115, 49158, 49229, 49410

Total: 24

30 January 1954

MR 2P 4–4–0	40443, 40461, 40552
LMS 2P 4–4–0	40646, 40678
LMS Fowler 2–6–4T	42309, 42320, 42345, 42346, 42347
LMS 3F 0–6–0T	47588, 47590, 47606, 47649, 47653, 47665
LNWR 0–8–0	49047, 49115, 49158, 49229, 49410

Total: 21

1959

LMS 2P 4–4–0	40583, 40646, 40678
LMS Fowler 2–6–4T	42309, 42347, 42389, 42400
LMS Stanier 2–6–4T	42425, 42562
LMS 3F 0–6–0T	47359, 47475, 47588, 47590, 47649, 47653, 47665
LNWR 0–8–0	48943, 49081, 49115, 49126, 49198, 49357, 49410, 49446

Total: 24

1965

LMS Fowler 2–6–4T	42381
LMS Stanier 'Class 5' 4–6–0	44813, 44963, 45110, 45147, 45374
LMS 3F 0–6–0T	47359, 47665
LMS 8F 2–8–0	48602

Total: 9

CHAPTER SEVEN

NATIONALIZATION

The new Labour government's proposal to nationalize the railways was met with vigorous opposition by the railway companies, the LMS even producing a cinema film attempting to explain the advantages of a privately owned railway. On the other hand, railway employees were very much in favour of state ownership and greeted eventual state control with enthusiasm. Once the 1947 Transport Act came into effect, on 1 January 1948, the old LMS system survived intact in England and Wales, but its Scottish operations were merged with those of the LNER to form a new Scottish Region. The remainder of the system, including Stafford, became the new BR London–Midland Region, with its headquarters at Euston.

While still in private ownership the LMS embarked on an experiment in diesel-electric traction, following the company's success with 0–6–0 diesel shunters during the pre-war years, when CME H.A. Ivatt worked in conjunction with the English-Electric company to produce two 1Co–Co1 locomotives which were to be the forerunners of modern main line diesel-electric locomotives. The first, No. 10000, emerged early in 1948 as a BR machine. These two locos worked double-headed on the West Coast Main Line on Glasgow–Euston expresses passing through Stafford. The station also saw Southern Region diesel-electric loco No. 10202 on the 'Royal Scot' service during 1952, this being one of three built at Ashford.

The new BR, with CME R.A. Riddles, had to retain a commitment to steam traction because of insufficient capital to undertake railway electrification on a large scale, and there was a lack of 'hard currency' to purchase foreign oil to power diesel locomotives. To assess the best features of the pre-nationalization loco stock, which were to be incorporated on the new 'Standard' steam loco fleet, interchange trials were organized in 1948. These trials brought ex-LNER A4 Pacific, 60034 *Lord Faringdon* and ex-SR 'Merchant Navy' Pacific No. 35017 *Belgian Marine* to the West Coast main line, on the Euston–Carlisle section of Glasgow expresses, running via the Trent Valley line and Stafford. These engines made an unusual sight in the heart of ex-LMS territory.

Results of the interchange trials proved inconclusive but BR pressed on with designs for its 'Standard' locomotives and by March 1949 requirements had been outlined. The first of the new 'Standards' to appear were the 'Britannia' Pacifics, No. 70000, *Britannia* herself, emerging from nearby Crewe works on 2 January 1951. The Class appeared regularly at Stafford from 1953 when it replaced ex-LMS 'Royal Scots' on the 'Irish Mail'. Following the introduction of the new Pacifics, the first few years of the 1950s saw 'Standard' Class 5 4–6–0s, 'Standard' Class 4 2–6–4 tanks, and 9F 2–10–0s become an increasingly common sight on express, semi-fast, local and freight trains at Stafford, although ex-LMS types were still predominant right up until the end of steam.

Ex-LMS Class 5 4–6-0 No. 45130 waits at Stafford station with a Birmingham-bound train on 13 November 1956. (*H.F. Wheeller Collection/Roger Carpenter*)

After wartime neglect, the new LM Region made modernization investment in its system, Stafford benefiting with the opening of a new signal-box, and then installation of colour light signalling in 1952. At the north end of the station a new 'No. 5' signal-box was built to replace the old one directly opposite. The new box controlled the Up and Down fast and slow lines at the north end of the station, and the junctions between the main lines, as well as the branches to Wellington and Stafford Common. In conjunction with this the layout at Stafford was remodelled to improve operations and the old box was taken out of use. Multiple aspect colour light signalling was installed on the main line, controlled by the new box, and track circuiting was also introduced, all of which was designed to improve working of trains in poor weather conditions.

Ex-LNWR Class 6F 0–8–0 No. 49359 of Bescot shed, leaving Stafford with a northbound goods train on 23 June 1951. The imposing gantry of LNWR signals, guarding the approach to Stafford station, may be seen in the distance. (*P. Kendrick; F.W. Shuttleworth Collection*)

THE MERSEYSIDE EXPRESS

LIVERPOOL (Lime Street) and LONDON (Euston)

	Week- days am			Week- days pm
Liverpool (Lime Street) .... dep	10 0	London (Euston) .... dep	6 5
	pm	Mossley Hill .. .. arr	9B48
London (Euston) .. ..arr	1A45	Liverpool (Lime Street) .... „	10 6

Restaurant Car Train

A—On Saturdays arrives London (Euston) 1 52 pm.   **B**—On Saturdays arrives Mossley Hill 9 52 pm.

Seats on these trains are reservable in advance for passengers travelling from London (Euston), Manchester (London Road), and Liverpool (Lime Street) on payment of fee of 1/- per seat.

A timetable for 'The Merseyside Express', mid-1950s. Like freight, the majority of the population used the railways to travel long distances, but, as the motorway network spread and private ownership of cars increased during the 1960s, passengers deserted the railways in vast numbers, not least because of the dilapidated state of the system, following wartime neglect, and continued use of steam traction which was perceived by the general public as dirty and slow. (*Author's Collection*)

Ex-Great Western Railway 'Castle' Class 4–6–0 No. 5015 *Kingswear Castle* heads the 9 a.m. Birkenhead–Paddington express through Stafford, Sunday 29 November 1953. This was an unusual sight on this LNWR route, and due to rebuilding work on the ex-GWR Shrewsbury–Wolverhampton line at Shifnal. The train will head to Wolverhampton on the former GJR route to Bushbury and regain the GWR line at Bushbury Junction, Wolverhampton to Wolverhampton (Low Level) station. This was not, however, the first time that GWR engines had appeared at Stafford. In 1910, a GWR 'Star' Class 4–6–0 operated over the LNWR from Euston to Crewe while the GWR took Experiment Class 4–6–0 No. 1471 *Worcestershire* for trials. GWR loco *Polar Star* (No. 4005) ran over the LNWR between 15 and 27 August 1910 and proved to be the master of any work it was given. Another GWR 'Castle' Class 4–6–0, No. 5000 *Launceston Castle*, was loaned to the new LMS in November 1926, in order for the new company to evaluate locomotive needs as the engines then in use were not powerful enough to meet the demands of its Scottish services. No. 5000 proved more than adequate for the demands placed upon it. So impressed were the LMS that they asked Swindon if they would build some Castles for them, but they declined and the Euston company was forced to seek solutions for themselves, which culminated in the construction of the famous 'Royal Scot' Class 4–6–0, designated by the LMS when preparing drawings as 'improved Castle type'. Other unusual locomotives appeared at Stafford over the years, including ex-LNER A4 Pacific No. 60034 *Lord Faringdon* and ex-SR 'Merchant Navy' Class Pacific No. 35017 *Belgian Marine*, as part of Locomotive Exchange Trials in 1948 to establish a new BR 'Standard' steam locomotive. (*Roger Carpenter*)

Ex-LMS Standard Compound 4–4–0 No. 41060 in black livery with LNWR style lining, and with chimney covered, lies stored at the side of Stafford station on 26 February 1955. (*P. Kendrick; F.W. Shuttleworth Collection*)

On 23 September 1955, ex-LMS 4–4–0 No. 41060, no longer in store, is seen in steam at the station platform, while ex-MR 4–4–0 No. 40447 is now stored in an adjacent siding. (*P. Kendrick; F.W. Shuttleworth Collection*)

Ex-LMS 'Patriot' Class 4–6–0 No. 45515 *Caernarvon* waits at Stafford station with its train, possibly from Llandudno, 13 November 1956. The fireman may be preparing to move coal forward in the tender. The train appears to be made up of non-corridor stock and was probably the 4 p.m. from Llandudno to Birmingham (New Street). This train was usually on time when it left Crewe, but thereafter became late because the Liverpool and Manchester to Euston expresses, running ahead of the Llandudno train, had to stop at Stafford, which this train often did not have to do. For this reason, it was occasionally forced to crawl 'wrong line' along the station, avoiding the loop behind Stafford station, which made it late at Wolverhampton. With a ticket stop at Dudley Port (New Street being an 'open' station at that time) so that tickets could be collected before arrival at New Street, the train could be as much as half an hour late into Birmingham. (*H.F. Wheeller Collection/Roger Carpenter*)

THE MANCUNIAN

MANCHESTER (London Road) and LONDON (Euston)

	Week-days am		Week-days pm
Manchester (London Road)......... dep. 9 45		London (Euston) .... dep 6 0	
	pm	Wilmslow .. .. .. arr 9 18	
London (Euston) .. .. .. arr 1 23		Manchester (London Road) .... ,, 9 45	

Restaurant Car Train

A timetable for 'The Mancunian', which ran between Euston and Manchester (London Road), via Stafford. (*Author's Collection*)

Ex-MR 2P 4–4–0 No. 40461 waits at Stafford station, 13 November 1956. Note the MR tender on this engine, which gives away its parentage. Also, the station roof appears to be falling into disrepair and will disappear, along with the rest of the station buildings, in the next six years when the line is electrified. (*H.F. Wheeller Collection/Roger Carpenter*)

Ex-MR 4–4–0, No. 40332 in store at the side of Stafford station, 2 April 1956. (*P. Kendrick; F.W. Shuttleworth Collection*)

Week Days

Miles	Station		
	LONDON (Euston)......dep		
5¼	Willesden Junction.....,,		
17½	Watford Junction.....,,		
20¼	King's Langley A.....,,		
22½	Apsley.....,,		
24½	Hemel Hempsted B.....,,		
27	Berkhamsted C.....,,		
31½	Tring D.....,,		
35½	Cheddington.....,,		
65	LUTON (E.R.).....dep		
40½	Leighton Buzzard.....arr		
46¾	Bletchley.....arr		
64	CAMBRIDGE.....dep		
66	OXFORD (Rewley Rd).....,,		
68	BANBURY (Merton St).....,,		
	Bletchley.....dep		
52	Wolverton F.....,,		
54	Castlethorpe.....,,		
59	Roade.....,,		
62½	Blisworth.....,,		
65½	70 Northampton (Castle) {arr / dep}		
71¼	Althorp Park.....,,		
75¼	Long Buckby.....,,		
80¾	Kilsby and Crick.....,,		
	Blisworth.....dep		
69¾	Weedon.....,,		
75¾	Welton.....,,		
82½	Rugby.....arr		
92¼	71 LEAMINGTON SPA 73.....arr		
	75 Rugby.....dep		
94	75 Coventry.....,,		
112¾	75 Birmingham (N. St.).....,,		
117	77 Walsall.....,,		
121¾	76 Dudley.....,,		
125¾	76 Wolverhampton.....,,		
	71 LEAMINGTON SPA 73.....dep		
	73 COVENTRY 75.....,,		
	Rugby.....dep		
88	Brinklow, for Stretton.....,,		
91¼	Shilton.....[under-Fosse]		
97	Nuneaton (Trent Val.).....,,		
227	LEICESTER (Lon. Rd.).....dep		
	Nuneaton (Trent Val.).....dep		
102¾	Atherstone.....,,		
106½	Polesworth.....,,		
110	Tamworth (Low Level).....,,		
116½	Lichfield (Trent Valley) {dep}		
121	Armitage.....,,		
127½	Rugeley (Trent Valley).....,,		
127½	Colwich.....,,		
129½	Milford and Brocton G.....,,		
133¼	Stafford.....arr		

	75 LEAMINGTON SPA.....dep		
	75 COVENTRY.....,,		
	76 Birmingham (N. St.).....,,		
	77 WALSALL 84.....,,		
	76 DUDLEY.....,,		
	76 WOLVERHAMPTON.....,,		
	76 Stafford.....,,		
162½	88 SHREWSBURY.....arr		
	Stafford.....dep		
136	Great Bridgeford (Closed).....,,		
138½	Norton Bridge J.....,,		
146	STOKE-ON-TRENT.....arr		
165½	MACCLESFIELD K 125.....,,		
143	Standon Bridge.....,,		
147½	Whitmore.....,,		
150½	Madeley.....,,		
158	Crewe.....arr		
	118 Crewe.....dep		
181½	118 STOCKPORT.....,,		
192½	140 Manchester (Vic.).....,,		
187	118 ,, (L. Rd.).....,,		
207	146 HUDDERSFIELD.....,,		
	139 Crewe.....dep		
193½	139 LIVERPOOL (Lime St.).....,,		
	BELFAST.....,,		
	99 Crewe.....dep		
179½	99 Chester (General).....arr		
194½	99 BIRKENHEAD (W.).....,,		
209½	99 RHYL.....,,		
219½	99 COLWYN BAY.....,,		
227	99 LLANDUDNO.....,,		
239	99 BANGOR.....,,		
263½	99 HOLYHEAD.....,,		
333½	Dublin (Westl'd Rw).....,,		
	Crewe.....dep		
182½	Warrington (Bank Q.).....arr		
192	149 St. Helens.....arr		
194	Wigan (N.W.).....,,		
211½	148 SOUTHPORT N.....,,		
209	Preston.....,,		
227	160 BLACKPOOL (North).....,,		
225½	160 ,, (Cen.).....,,		
229½	160 FLEETWOOD.....,,		
230	Lancaster (Castle).....,,		
234	51 MORECAMBE (Eus. Rd).....,,		
237½	51 HEYSHAM.....,,		
349½	BELFAST.....,,		
265	195 BARROW.....arr		
259½	202 WINDERMERE.....,,		
281	Penrith X.....,,		
296½	202 KESWICK.....,,		
299	Carlisle.....arr		
400	EDINBRO' (Prin. St.).....arr		
401½	GLASGOW (Central).....,,		
456	PERTH (General).....,,		
471	DUNDEE (West).....,,		
539½	ABERDEEN.....,,		
568	INVERNESS.....,,		

A 1955 timetable for express services between Euston, the north-west of England, North Wales and Scotland, with all trains running via Stafford. (*Author's Collection*)

Table 12

Table 12

THE LAKES EXPRESS

THROUGH RESTAURANT CAR EXPRESS TRAIN

BETWEEN

LONDON AND THE LAKE DISTRICT

WEEKDAYS

		noon					am	am
London (Euston) .... dep		12 0		Workington (Main) .... dep			8 35	....
		pm		Brigham .. .. ,,			8 54	....
Wigan (North Western) { arr		3 53		Cockermouth‡ .... ,,			9 2	....
dep		3 57		Bassenthwaite Lake .. .. ,,			9 13	..
Preston .... { arr		4 22		Braithwaite .... ,,			9 21	..
dep		4 26		Keswick .. .. ,,			9 38	....
Lancaster (Castle) .. { arr		4 55		Penrith* .... ,,			10 24	....
dep		4 57		Tebay .. .. ,,			11 0	..
arr		5 22						
Oxenholme .... {				Windermere¶ .... dep			....	10 50
dep	5 27	5 35		Staveley .. .. ,,			..	10 59
				Burneside .... ,,			....	11 4
Kendal.. .. .. .. arr	..	5 39		Kendal.. .. .. ,,			..	11 13
Burneside .... ,,	....	5 46						
Staveley .. .. .. ,,	..	5 55		Oxenholme .... { arr			11 17	11 19
Windermere¶ .... ,,	....	6 5						
				dep			11 30	
Penrith* .. .. arr	6 16	..		Carnforth .. .. { arr			11 46	
Blencow .... ,,	6 34	....		dep			11 50	
Penruddock .. .. .. ,,	6 43	..					pm	
Troutbeck† .... ,,	6 48	....		Lancaster .... { arr			12 0	
Threlkeld .. .. .. ,,	6 56	....		dep			12 5	
Keswick .... ,,	7 5	....		arr			12 35	
Braithwaite .. .. .. ,,	7 31	....					SX	SO
Bassenthwaite Lake .... ,,	7 40	....		Preston .. .. .. {			pm	pm
Embleton .. .. .. ,,	7 46	..					12 45	12 43
Cockermouth‡ .... ,,	7 52	....		Wigan (North Western) .... { dep			1 11	—
Brigham .. .. ,,	7 59	....		arr			1 16	—
Camerton .. .. .. ,,	8 6	....		Warrington (Bank Quay) { dep			1 38	—
Workington Bridge .. .. ,,	8 15	..		arr			1 43	—
Workington (Main) .... ,,	8 20	....		Crewe .... { dep			2 15	1 58
				arr			2 24	2 8
				London (Euston) .. .. .. arr			5 21	5 9

NOTES

SO—Saturdays only.
SX—Saturdays excepted.

*—Station for Ullswater Lake (Pooley Bridge) (5¾ miles).
†—Station for Ullswater Lake (5¾ miles).
‡—Station for Buttermere.
¶—Station for Bowness (1¼ miles) and Ambleside (4¼ miles).

Restaurant Car and Through Carriages between London and Windermere. Through Carriages between London and Workington via Keswick.

Seats on these trains are reservable in advance for passengers travelling from London (Euston), Windermere and Workington (Main) on payment of fee of 1/- per seat.

A 1950s timetable for 'The Lakes Express', the train running from Euston and serving resorts in the Lake District, Cumberland. (*Author's Collection*)

Ex-LMS 'Patriot' Class 4–6–0 No. 45520 *Llandudno* is seen departing from Stafford station with a Birmingham (New Street) express, late 1950s. (*Roger Carpenter*)

BR 'Standard' Class 5 4–6–0 No. 73093 stands at Stafford station at the head of a passenger train, late 1950s. As a result of the 1948 Interchange Trials, BR 'Standard' types appeared at Stafford from 1953 when 'Britainnia' Pacifics replaced ex-LMS 'Royal Scot' 4–6–0s on 'Irish Mail' trains. From that time, new 'Standard' class 4 and 5 4–6–0s, 2–6–4 tanks, and Class 9F 2–10–0s became an increasingly common sight at Stafford. (*Roger Carpenter*)

Ex-LMS 'Princess Coronation' Class Pacific No. 46248 *City of Leeds* is approaching Stafford No. 5 signal-box with an Up express for Euston on the fast line. On the right is a timber yard, while Bagnall's locoworks can be glimpsed on the left, just before the branch to Wellington. (*Author's Collection*)

THE WELSHMAN
THROUGH RESTAURANT CAR EXPRESS TRAIN BETWEEN LONDON and NORTH WALES
WEEKDAYS

Table II · Table 11

	Mondays to Fridays		Saturdays only	
	am		am	
London (Euston) .... dep	11 15		11 15	
	pm		pm	
Rugby (L.M.R.) .. .. .. „	12 54		12 57	
Crewe .. .. .. „	2 37		....	
Beeston Castle .. .. „	2 53		....	
Chester (General) .. .. { arr	3 8		3 8	
Chester (General) .. .. { dep	3 15	3 23	3 15	3 23
Prestatyn .. .. arr	....	3 55	....	3 56
Rhyl .. .. „	....	4 2	....	4 4
Abergele .. .. „	....	4 13	....	4 17
Colwyn Bay .. .. .. „	....	4 25	....	4 30
Llandudno Junction .... „	....	4 33	....	4 38
Deganwy .. .. arr	..	4 41	..	4 48
Llandudno .... „	....	4 46	....	4 53
Penmaenmawr .. .. .. arr	4 12	....	4 12	..
Llanfairfechan .... „	4 20	....	4 20	....
Bangor.. .. .. „	4 31	....	4 31	....
Menai Bridge .. .. .. „	4 44	....	4 44	....
Port Dinorwic .. .. .. „	4 50	....	4 50	....
Caernarvon .. .. .. „	4 59	....	4 59	....
Penygroes .. .. „	5 22	....	5 22	....
Brynkir .. .. „	5 35	....	5 35	....
Chwilog .. .. „	5 46	....	5 46	....
Afonwen .. .. „	5 50	....	5 50	....
Pwllheli .. .. arr	6 10	..	6 10	..
Criccieth .. .. arr	6 3	..	6 3	....
Portmadoc .. .. „	6 12	..	6 12	....

	Mondays to Fridays	Saturdays only
	am	am
Portmadoc .. .. dep	.. 11 0	.. 9 55
Criccieth .... „	.. 11 9	.... 10 4
Pwllheli .. .. dep	.. 11 0	10 0
Afonwen ....dep	.... 11 25	.... 10 25
Chwilog .. .. „	.. 11 29	10 29
Brynkir .... „	.. 11 42	.... 10 42
Penygroes .. .. „	.. 11 54	.... 10 54
Groeslon .... „	.. 11 58	.... 10 58
	pm	
Caernarvon .. .. .. „	12 16	11 16
Menai Bridge .. .. .. „	.. 12 28	.. 11 28
Bangor .. .. „	.. 12 45	.. 11 45
Llanfairfechan .... „	.. 12 56	.. 11 57
		pm
Penmaenmawr .. .. .. „	pm 1 3	pm 12 5
Llandudno .... dep	1 0	12 14
Deganwy .. .. .. „	1 5	..
Llandudno Junction .... dep	1 24	12 34
Colwyn Bay .. .. .. „	1 32	12 45
Rhyl.. .. .. „	1 51	1 7
Prestatyn .. .. „	1 59	....
Chester (General) .... „	2 40	1 53
Beeston Castle .. .. „	2 58	....
Crewe .. .. arr	3 15	....
Stafford .. .. .. „	3 56	
London (Euston) .... „	6 28	5 34

Through Carriages between London and Llandudno, Pwllheli, Portmadoc.
Restaurant Car between London and Bangor.

A 1950s timetable for 'The Welshman' from Euston to North Wales. This train ran complete to Prestatyn where it divided, one half running to Llandudno, while the other half ran to Bangor from where a tank loco took the train down the Caernarfon branch to Afon Wen on the GWR Cambrian Coast line. At Afon Wen the train divided again, one half going to Portmadoc and the other half going to Pwllheli. This train was very much a holiday service and only ran in the summer months. (*Author's Collection*)

99

Ex-LMS Stanier 2–6–0 No. 42968 entering Stafford station, 6 May 1959. This is a local train from Wellington, the latter station being jointly owned with the GWR. At Wellington connections could be made with Paddington–Birkenhead services for Chester, Shrewsbury (for the Cambrian Coast line), Birkenhead (Woodside), Wolverhampton (Low Level) and Birmingham (Snow Hill). (*H.F. Wheeller Collection/Roger Carpenter*)

The Up 'Red Rose' from Liverpool to Euston, with ex-LMS Class 5 4–6–0 No. 44907 and ex-LMS 'Patriot' Class 4–6–0 No. 45551 in charge, 6 May 1959. After leaving Stafford this train will run on to Euston. (*H.F. Wheeller Collection/Roger Carpenter*)

Hauling the Up 'Midday Scot', from Glasgow to Euston through Stafford, is ex-LMS 'Princess-Coronation' Pacific No. 46229 *Duchess of Hamilton*, 6 May 1959. (*H.F. Wheeller Collection/ Roger Carpenter*)

THE ROYAL SCOT
LONDON (Euston) and GLASGOW (Central)

WEEKDAYS

				am						am
London (Euston)	..	..	..dep	10 0	Glasgow (Central)	..	..	..dep	10 0
				pm						pm
Glasgow (Central)	..	..	..arr	6 25	London (Euston)	..	..	..arr	6 13

Restaurant Car Train

THE MID-DAY SCOT
LONDON (Euston) and GLASGOW (Central)

WEEKDAYS

				pm					pm
London (Euston) ..	..	..	..dep	1 0	Glasgow (Central)	..	..	..dep	1 15
Rugby (L.M.R.) ..	..	..	.. ,,	2 37	Motherwell	..	..	.. ,,	1 36
Crewe ..	..	..	.. ,,	4 14	Carstairs ..	..	..	.. ,,	2A24
Carlisle ..	..	..	..arr	7 17	Carlisle	..	..	.. ,,	3B50
Carstairs ..	..	..	.. ,,	8 56	Crewe	..	..	.. arr	6 59
Motherwell ..	..	..	.. ,,	9 23	Watford Junction	..	..	.. ,,	9 40
Glasgow (Central)	..	..	.. ,,	9 45	London (Euston) ..	..	..	.. ,,	10 10

Restaurant Car Train.

A—Does not call at Carstairs on Saturdays from June 17th to August 26th inclusive.
B—On Saturdays June 17th to August 26th inclusive departs Carlisle 3 31 pm.

Timetables for the 'Royal Scot' and 'Midday Scot', 1950s. (*Author's Collection*)

Ex-LMS Stanier 2–6–2 tank engine No. 40122 on station pilot duties at Stafford station in the late 1950s. (*Roger Carpenter*)

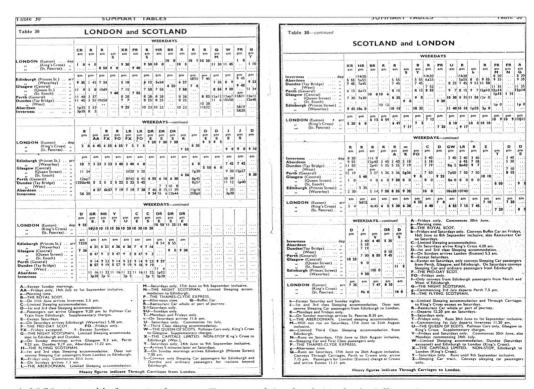

A 1950s timetable for trains between Euston and Scotland. (*Author's Collection*)

The south bay starting signals at Stafford station, 6 May 1959. (*H.F. Wheeller Collection/ Roger Carpenter*)

Stafford No. 4 signal-box, 26 February 1988. This box is similar to the No. 5 box built by British Railways London Midland Region in 1952, in conjunction with installation of colour light signalling at the station. The new No. 5 box was built at the north end of the station, replacing the old one directly opposite. The new box controlled the Up and Down fast lines, and the slow lines at the north end of the station. The box also controlled the junctions between the main lines and the branches to Wellington and Stafford Common. In conjunction with the installation of the new box, the layout at Stafford station was remodelled to improve operations. The old box with its 123-lever frame had become uneconomical to maintain and could not be altered to operate the new layout. Multiple aspect colour light signalling was also installed on the main line, which was controlled by the new box, which had a mechanical 150-lever frame, and track circuiting was also introduced, all of which was designed to improve working of trains in poor weather conditions. Only three years after the opening of the new No. 5 signal-box the government approved a capital expenditure of £1,240 million on the whole of the British railway system, which was to bring electrification to Stafford, along with a completely new station. (*Revd D. Hardy*)

CHAPTER EIGHT

BAGNALL'S LOCOMOTIVE WORKS

As well as being the location for the main line railway, station and locoshed, Stafford was also the home of W.G. Bagnall, builders of industrial and main locos which were exported all over the world. Its Castle Engine Works, opened in 1875, were situated on the Down side of the LNWR main line to Crewe between Stafford station and the junction with the Shropshire Union Railway and Canal Company's line to Wellington. Though not a major loco builder, the works being rather small and somewhat primitive, the company's products became well known throughout the world, achieving as much fame as those from much larger firms such as Beyer-Peacock, Robert Stephenson and the North British Locomotive Company. Even at its peak the company employed only some 350–400 men and the works was always rather old-fashioned, most machinery being belt driven, while it always suffered from a lack of investment in modern equipment.

In its early days Bagnall's specialized in small narrow gauge locos for railway contractors, after coming late into the market. Over the years the company went on to patent its own valve gear, circular fireboxes (Bagnall's being the only company to use them as standard on a large scale) and inverted saddle tanks. The company was also involved in general railway engineering and construction of rolling stock.

William Gordon Bagnall, who had gained engineering experience at his uncle's firm of John Bagnall & Sons Ltd, Ironfounders, of Wolverhampton, established the W.G. Bagnall Company in 1875 when he acquired a small millwrights business in Castle Town, Stafford. The millwrights factory had been established in 1870 by Massey and Hill, on land leased from Lord Stafford, employing about fifty men and boys in a works that consisted of one building approximately 200 ft × 25 ft. It was in this works that Bagnall's built the first of a long list of locomotives.

This first engine was a standard gauge 0–4–0, with 7⅜ in × 11 in cylinders and a 4 ft 6 in wheelbase. The loco had a copper firebox and brass tubes, carrying Bagnall's list number of 16. It was built without a customer and took only seven months to erect, being completed in 1876. The engine eventually went to the Duke of Buckingham's newly opened Wotton Tramway in Buckinghamshire, where two Aveling and Porter geared locos were proving to be inadequate for the work expected of them. On hearing of Wotton Tramway's problems, Bagnall offered to hire his first loco for trials there, an offer that the Duke gratefully accepted, and No. 16, now named *Buckingham*, was sent to Quainton Road station, the starting point of the tramway, in December 1876. No. 16 was quite successful and the Duke ordered a similar but larger loco. *Buckingham* was later sold by Bagnall to a

A rake of 2–4–2 tank locomotives are lined up on flat wagons outside the locoworks, the chimneys and roofs of which are visible in the right background, in the 1930s. They are awaiting export to the Indian subcontinent where most of the company's products were sent. Unlike other loco builders, Bagnall's remained fairly busy during the 1930s Depression. While other firms went bankrupt Bagnall's managed to secure several large orders and at the height of the economic slump the company's employees never worked less than a three-day week, those employed there being seen as comparatively well off by the local population. (*Allan Baker*)

contractor, and the company had 'arrived' in the private locomotive-building business.

Bagnall's remained as an independent company until it was sold to the Stafford engineering company of W.H. Dorman & Co. on 27 January 1959, the Castle Works still busy with a full order book. Dorman's were builders of diesel engines, which allowed the Castle Works to build diesel locos. However, the fortunes of the old Bagnall works was to take a turn for the worse when Dorman's was taken over by the giant English Electric Company (now GEC). English Electric embarked on a programme of 'asset stripping' the Bagnall works by transferring loco building, including a large order for Sudan, to Robert Stephenson and Hawthorn of Darlington, which itself had only recently fallen into the English Electric net. Only locos in advanced stages of production were allowed to be completed at Stafford and no new work was to be commenced. The Castle Works was finally closed in 1972, being deemed too small and surplus to requirements, after a life of eighty-six years.

The drawing office at Bagnall's, where many of the company's loco designs were produced; several of Bagnall's engines can be seen above the drawing boards. From 1887, Bagnall's became a limited company and the works underwent considerable expansion, eventually covering an area of 11 acres. At around the same time the company was beginning to win contracts for large locos and began specialising in fully equipped light railways: track, rolling stock, and locos. To assist in developing these light railways the company patented a portable 'permanent way' using pressed steel sleepers which did not require chairs, bolts or keys. This system became quite common on light railways all over the world. In 1891, Ernest Baguley joined Bagnall's from Hawthorn Leslie (another private loco builder) of Newcastle-upon-Tyne. He completely reorganized the firm on the lines of his former employers. He was also responsible for a locomotive design which typified Bagnall's, the narrow gauge saddle tank with circular firebox. The first of these was built in 1891, and the last in 1953. While there were many small differences in design, their parentage was never in doubt. (*Allan Baker*)

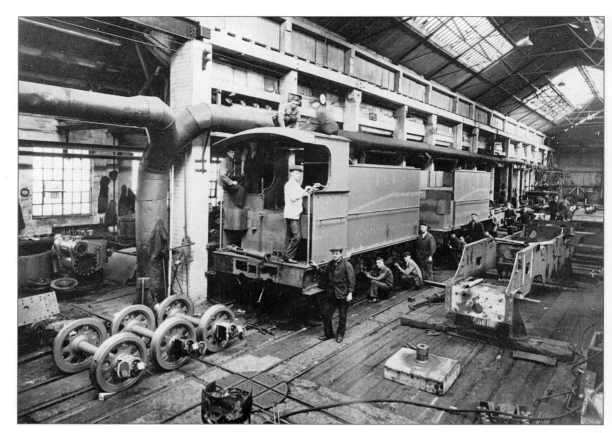

One of the production lines at Bagnall's, with tank locos for India under construction, 1950s. In the early twentieth century expansion of the works continued. Fortunately, the land leased from Lord Stafford was of sufficient size to accommodate these various extensions. The erecting shop, seen here and in the next picture, which was parallel to the LNWR main line, had several additions over the years, and each one could be traced by the different types of wood, steelwork and brickwork used. With increased capacity the company could accept large orders for bigger engines and nothing was rejected. Rolling stock orders also increased and a special shop was built for this work. As the company grew and orders increased its founder, W.G. Bagnall, died on 19 July 1907 at the age of fifty-five years, his health having deteriorated in his final few years. (*Allan Baker*)

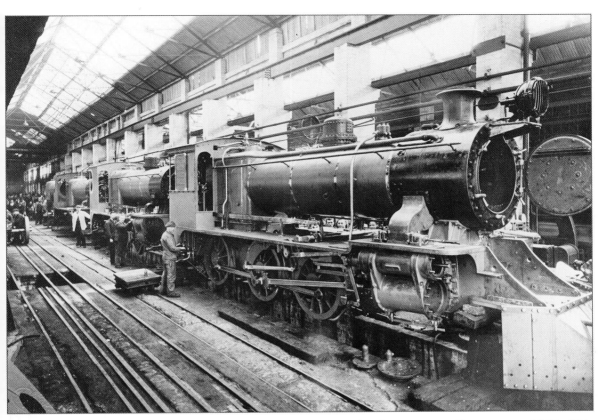

The erecting shop, with 2–6–0 tender engines under construction for the Egyptian railway system, 1950s. This was one of a number of large orders that the company undertook during the first half of the twentieth century. The First World War brought new work to Bagnall's when many 2 ft gauge locos, built by Baldwin & Alco of the USA, for war service in France were rebuilt or repaired. The company also produced and supplied a huge quantity of spares for these locos. After the war, the company had several of these engines on their hands which were rebuilt, regauged where necessary, and sold to various industrial users in Great Britain, Bagnall's also built several batches of their standard narrow gauge saddle tanks for the Ministry of Munitions, as well as doing munitions work in its own right. The return of peace saw the works completely retooled and modernized. The 1920s saw Bagnall's take on an order for a 3 ft 6 in gauge 0–4–0 saddle tank for the LNWR, their first ever order from an English main line railway company. This engine had the works number 2153 and cost the LNWR £3,275, being delivered to the Wolverton and Stony Stratford Railway on 27 October 1921. It was to be the forerunner of further orders from English main line railways. (*Allan Baker*)

Members of the management team on the footplate of newly built 2–6–0 No. 97 for Egyptian railways, 1950s. Every component, except copper and steel tubes, fireboxes and steel castings was fabricated at the works. Bagnall foundries only produced cast-iron and brass components. Locos for the home market were always moved by rail under their own steam, while export engines were transported by the LMS low loader wagons to the docks at Liverpool. (*Allan Baker*)

Bagnall's cricket team, 1950s. Like other companies, Bagnall's encouraged their employees to participate in sport as a way of building up team spirit which could be translated to everyday working activities. While wages were not the highest, a skilled fitter earning £5 7s a week at this time, Bagnall's looked after its employees. Those who were sick, with little or no prospect of returning to work, were kept on the payroll and paid statutory holiday pay. (*Allan Baker*)

Office and drawing office staff pose alongside 2–6–0 No. 97. Along with manual workers, staff members were also looked after. Any staff members who needed to attend hospital away from Stafford were always provided with a car to take them and salary was paid beyond the statutory twelve weeks. There were, however, some dangerous practices undertaken inside the works. For example, when new locos were being steam tested apprentices would go into the pit underneath the engine to adjust the cylinder cocks, risking possible scalding from steam. Apprentices were also required to mix asbestos powder with water and apply the paste under the cylinders for the cylinder cocks. Boiler lagging was also made of asbestos. It can only be imagined what the modern Health and Safety Executive would have made of such practices today. Despite the hazardous nature of locomotive construction in those days there were surprisingly few accidents. At the same time, Bagnall's works retained a family atmosphere and, like those of the main line companies, generation followed generation into the firm. Work was often dirty and heavy, with conditions being generally uncomfortable, usually very cold in winter and too hot in summer. In those days the apprenticeship system operated by the company was comprehensive. Most fitting and turning apprentices started off marking up and then graduated through the machine shop and fitting shop. (*Allan Baker*)

In 1925–6 Bagnall's received its first major order for the main line railway companies when the new LMS ordered twenty-five Class 3F 0–6–0 tank engines, with a further seven for the Somerset and Dorset Joint Railway, one of which, No. 23, is seen here. These were as follows:

Works No.	Running Nos	Delivery Dates
For LMS		
2288	16535/7452/47452	19 August 1926
2289	16536/7453/47453	28 August 1926
2290	16537/7454/47454	20 September 1926
2291	16538/7455/47455	25 September 1926
2292	16539/7456/No BR no.	29 September 1926
2293	16540/7457/47457	23 October 1926
2294	16541/7458/47458	28 October 1926
2295	16542/7459/47459	26 November 1926
2296	16543/7460/47460	29 November 1926
2297	16544/7461/47461	28 March 1927
2298	16545/7462/47462	5 April 1927
2299	16546/7463/47463	20 April 1927
2300	16547/7464/47464	28 April 1927
2301	16548/7465/47465	21 May 1927
2302	16549/7466/47466	15 June 1927

Each loco cost the LMS £3,330, total price for the order being £49,950. Total cost to Bagnall's was £59,102 6s 10d, representing a loss of £9,152 6s 10d, each loco actually costing £3,827 12s 7d to build, with a further £1,687 17s added to construction costs for patterns, blocks and tools.

2343	16675/7592/47592	18 August 1928
2344	16676/7593/47593	18 August 1928
2345	16677/7594/47594	6 September 1928
2346	16678/7595/47595	11 September 1928
2347	16679/7596/47596	21 September 1928
2348	16680/7597/47597	27 September 1928
2349	16681/7598/47598	1 November 1928
2350	16682/7599/47599	7 November 1928
2351	16683/7600/47600	13 November 1928
2352	16684/7601/47601	22 November 1928

These locos cost £3,025 each, the total price for ten being £30,250. Cost to Bagnall's was £33,100 19s 3d, a loss of £2,850 19s 3d. Each loco cost £3,310 1s 11d to build, including £630 1s 2d for tools and blocks. These ten were cheaper per unit than the first fifteen because patterns, etc., had already been produced for the first batch.

For S&DJR

2358	19/7150/7310/47310	27 December 1928
2359	20/7151/7311/47311	7 January 1929
2360	21/7152/7312/47312	15 January 1929
2361	22/7153/7313/47313	22 January 1929
2362	23/7154/7314/47314	29 January 1929
2363	24/7155/7315/47315	5 February 1929
2364	25/7156/7316/47316	12 February 1929

Price to S&DJR was £3,050 each, £21,350 for all seven. Cost to Bagnall's was £23,816 4s 4d, a loss of £2,466 4s 4d.

All of the LMS 3F tanks were sent to Crewe on completion, and at least one, No. 7599, was allocated to Stafford locoshed. The S&DJR engines went to Bath on completion. Of these LMS locos, No. 7456 (works No. 2292) was regauged to 5 ft 3 in and sent to Ireland, having been transferred to the Northern Counties Committee, Northern Ireland in 1944, and given the number 18. Loco No. 47313 (works No. 2361) was one of the last 3Fs to remain in service, being withdrawn from Westhouses MPD in June 1967. Bagnall's also supplied 100 coupling rod forgings to Hunslet of Leeds for similar locos that they were building. As these locos were built when unemployment was rising in Britain, the government would have encouraged the main line railway companies to order new engines from outside firms in an effort to keep men at work, and would have underwritten losses made by the constructing companies. (*Allan Baker*)

Along with the order for the LMS, Bagnall's also constructed 50 57XX Class 0–6–0 Pannier tanks, in two batches, for the Great Western Railway from 1930 to 1931. One of the first batch of these locos, No. 6721 in photographic grey, is pictured here. These engines and their delivery dates were as follows:

Works No.	Running No.	Delivery Date
Batch One		
2381	6700	4 February 1930
2382	6701	4 February 1930
2383	6702	12 February 1930
2384	6703	12 February 1930
2385	6704	28 February 1930
2386	6705	28 February 1930
2387	6706	28 March 1930
2388	6707	1 April 1930
2389	6708	17 April 1930
2390	6709	28 April 1930
2391	6710	23 May 1930
2392	6711	23 May 1930
2393	6712	6 June 1930
2394	6713	6 June 1930
2395	6714	17 June 1930
2396	6715	10 July 1930
2397	6716	22 July 1930
2398	6717	30 July 1930
2399	6718	1 August 1930
2400	6719	29 August 1930
2401	6720	8 September 1930
2402	6721	22 September 1930
2403	6722	25 September 1930

2404	6723	3 October 1930
2405	6724	3 October 1930

Batch Two

2422	8725	25 November 1930
2423	8726	5 December 1930
2424	8727	12 December 1930
2425	8728	19 December 1930
2426	8729	31 December 1930
2427	8730	30 January 1931
2428	8731	6 February 1931
2429	8732	13 February 1931
2430	8733	20 February 1931
2431	8734	27 February 1931
2432	8735	16 March 1931
2433	8736	23 March 1931
2434	8737	1 April 1931
2435	8738	13 April 1931
2436	8739	22 April 1931
2437	8740	11 May 1931
2438	8741	15 May 1931
2439	8742	22 May 1931
2440	8743	3 June 1931
2441	8744	11 June 1931
2442	8745	19 June 1931
2443	8746	25 June 1931
2444	8747	1 July 1931
2445	8748	8 July 1931
2446	8749	10 July 1931

The price of the first twenty-five locos to the GWR was £68,625, or £2,745 each. The cost to Bagnall's was £74,866 11s 7d, representing a loss of £6,241 11s 7d. The second batch were priced at £74,575 (£2,983 each) with a cost to Bagnall's of £70,891 13s 8d, a profit of £3,683 13s 8d, each loco costing an average of £2,835 13s 4d to build. These pannier tanks were delivered to Swindon, most of the first batch spending their working lives in the South Wales valleys. (*Allan Baker*)

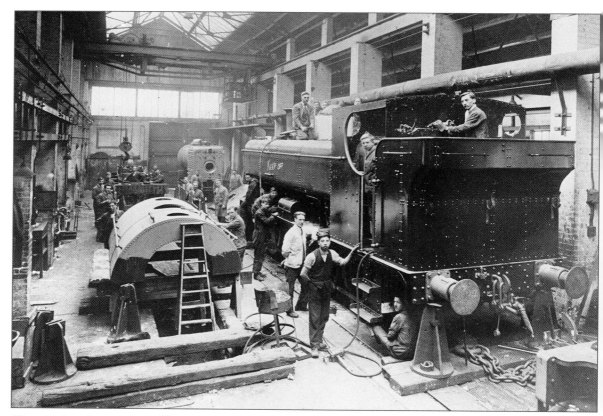

The erecting shop at Bagnall's in the 1930s, with construction of 57XX Class GWR 0–6–0 pannier tanks in progress. Fifty of Class 67XX pannier tanks were ordered by the GWR on the eve of nationalization, this being one of the last orders placed by a main line railway company to a private contractor. All were delivered to the new British Railways Western Region. The boilers for these engines were supplied by the GWR's Swindon works. The locos themselves had a very short working life, lasting a maximum of fifteen years, and some were actually withdrawn after running for only five years. The locos built by Bagnall's were as follows:

Works No.	Running No.	Delivery Date
2910	8400	27 July 1949
2911	8401	27 July 1949
2912	8402	24 August 1949
2913	8403	14 September 1949
2914	8404	15 September 1949
2915	8405	28 November 1949
2916	8406	29 November 1949
2917	8407	15 December 1949
2918	8408	19 December 1949
2919	8409	21 December 1949
2920	8410	29 December 1949
2921	8411	29 December 1949
2922	8412	30 December 1949
2923	8413	30 December 1949
2924	8414	31 December 1949
2925	8415	6 March 1950
2926	8416	7 March 1950
2927	8417	16 March 1950
2928	8418	23 March 1950
2929	8419	24 March 1950

2930	8420	3 September 1950
2931	8421	6 September 1950
2932	8422	26 September 1950
2933	8423	27 September 1950
2934	8424	21 November 1950
2935	8425	27 December 1950
2936	8426	29 December 1950
2937	8427	26 January 1951
2938	8428	31 December 1951
2939	8429	7 March 1952
2940	8430	30 December 1952
2941	8431	30 December 1952
2942	8432	13 February 1953
2943	8433	13 February 1953
2944	8434	23 February 1953
2945	8435	15 April 1953
2946	8436	22 April 1953
2947	8437	30 April 1953
2948	8438	20 May 1953
2949	8439	29 May 1953
2950	8440	25 February 1954
2951	8441	15 March 1954
2952	8442	19 March 1954
2953	8443	31 March 1954
2954	8444	22 April 1954
2955	8445	2 June 1954
2956	8446	14 June 1954
2957	8447	17 June 1954
2958	8448	23 June 1954
2959	8449	2 July 1954

The first twenty-five locos cost Western Region £216,825 (£8,673 each), the next five cost £44,604 (£8,920 16s), the five after cost £49,766 (£9,953 4s), and the final fifteen cost £151,776 (£10,118 8s), a total for the whole contract of £362,971. Profit to Bagnall's was £18,063. The final batch of five attracted a loss of £2,964, the profit on the first forty-five being £21,027. Much of the loss on the last five was due to price increases on raw materials (from £2,482 for the first loco to £4,156 for the last) and wage costs (from £1,942 for each of the first five engines to £2,071 for each of the last five). (*Allan Baker*)

Along with locomotives, Bagnall's was also involved in wagon construction. Here, at an unknown location, are examples of the company's tipper wagons used in quarries and coal mines. (*Allan Baker*)

A flat wagon, also built by Bagnall's. The automatic coupling suggests that it was built for the export market. (*Allan Baker*)

Little 0–4–0 tank loco *Ajax*, an example of the small engines built by Bagnall's for use on industrial railways. By 1933, the company had entered into diesel locomotive construction when Bagnall's formed an agreement with the German manufacturer, Deutz, to build, under licence, Deutz diesel locos using imported Deutz engines. Several of these were constructed until the outbreak of the Second World War brought an abrupt end to the supply of diesel engines. The company also designed a diesel loco of its own, a double-bogie articulated machine for use in mines. It was fitted with a Gardner engine and had a Bagnall-designed epicyclic gearbox. Entry into diesel loco construction was a natural progression for Bagnall's as it had been building petrol and electric engines for many years. Their first electric engine had been a four-wheeled vehicle for the City and South London Railway and was built as early as 1895. The first petrol loco was built in 1911. During the Second World War, Bagnall's undertook several large government contracts for wartime equipment, including the complete fitting out of standard gauge mobile workshop trains for service abroad. Along with several other builders the company built fifty-two standard gauge Ministry of Supply Hunslet 0–6–0 'Austerity' saddle tanks, at a cost to the ministry of £4,950 each. (*Allan Baker*)

After the war Bagnall's prospered, undertaking large orders for India and Egypt and, in 1947, the company was sold to a Mr A.P. Good who had interests in, among others, the Brush Electrical Engineering Company. Stafford shared in many joint ventures with Brush, including several batches of Type 2, later Class 24, diesel-electric locos for British Railways. In addition, Bagnall's built shunting engines for the Steel Company of Wales and twenty-five double-bogie locos for Ceylon. The company also diversified into general engineering, producing gun carriages for the War Office and industrial pressure vessels. At the same time, orders for steam locos were decreasing rapidly. The last new steam loco, a 2 ft gauge 2–8–2 with double-bogie tender for the Mysore Iron and Steel Company, was dispatched on 15 July 1957 and sold for £24,140 but cost £26,142 to build (a loss of £2,002). The last new locos of any sort were three 204 hp 0–6–0 diesel-mechanical engines (works Nos 3147–3149) for the National Coal Board. Ordered on 28 February 1958, they were all delivered by February 1960. The contract was worth £45,177, but building costs were £47,172. The company supplied fifty-eight sets of bogies, underframes and mechanical parts for A1A–A1A Type 2 diesel-electric locos (Class 31) then being built by Brush for British Railways, the contract being worth some £561,951 to Bagnall's. Although loco building had all but ceased, Bagnall's held contracts for repairs, which included three ex-Western Region 15XX 0–6–0 pannier tanks with outside valve gear which had been purchased by the National Coal Board and used at Coventry Colliery. One of these engines, still with its GWR number of 1501, is seen here at Coventry Colliery. (*Author's Collection*)

Bagnall's fortunes declined after English Electric took them over. Most Bagnall staff transferred to the GEC works in the town and all assets were stripped away, with all orders being sent to other works until the Castle Works was run down, finally closing in 1972 after a life of eighty-six years. In that time, some 1,869 locos had been built and some are preserved or are still working as testimonial to their quality. One such is *Isabel*, a little 0–4–0 saddle tank, seen here outside the works on 26 February 1955. Formerly owned by Markfield Granite Co. of Leicester, it was built in February 1897 (works No. 1491) and returned to Castle Works in March 1952. It was mechanically rebuilt by apprentices and mounted on a plinth in the works yard during Coronation year (1953), as a memorial to the men who had designed and built Bagnall locos over the years. When Bagnall's closed, the loco was moved to Victoria Park, Stafford (opposite the railway station). She returned to Castle Works for repaint in 1977 prior to the Silver Jubilee celebrations and was the last loco to receive attention at the works. Having been returned to its plinth, the loco suffered from the weather and the attention of vandals. She was later restored and is now on permanent display at the railway station. (*P. Kendrick; F.W. Shuttleworth Collection*)

Preserved Bagnall Locomotives

While none of the main line locos built by Bagnall's survived into preservation, several industrial types still exist. The full list is produced below, showing their original owners and the price paid for them when new, giving an idea of what the average Bagnall loco cost at the time.

1. Austerity 0–6–0ST

Date Built	Works No.	Running No./Name	Original Owner	Price
1944	2746	75158/144	War Dept	£4,950
1944	2749	75161	War Dept	£4,950
1944	2758	75170	War Dept	£4,950
1944	2759	75171/147/No. 16	War Dept	£4,950
1944	2766	75178	War Dept	£4,950
1945	2777	75254/No. 7	War Dept	£4,950
1945	2779	75256/Gamma	War Dept	£4,950

2. Industrial Locos

0–4–0ST

1931	2450	*J T Daly*	Horseley Bridge & Eng. Co. Ltd	£1,185
1932	2469	*Scott*	Fraser & Chalmers	£1,070
1936	2542	*Jubilee*	Edward Lloyd Ltd	£1,400
1936	2565		Northampton Electric Light Co.	£1,370
1937	2572	*Judy*	Port of Par Ltd	£1,200
1940	2623	*Hawarden*	Shelton & Co.	£5,656
1941	2648	*Linda*	Ministry of Supply	£2,700
1943	2702	*Matthew Murray*	Firth & Brown Ltd	£2,243
1946	2842	*No. 2 Hampshire*	London Electric Supply Co.	£3,570
1950	2962	No. 19	The Admiralty	£5,791
1953	3058	*Alfred*	Selleck Nicholls & Co. Ltd	£6,118

0–6–0PT

1940	2613	*Brookfield*	The Admiralty	£2,617

0–6–0ST

1922	2193	*Topham*	Edward Lloyd Ltd	£2,635
1927	2221	*Lewisham*	Shropshire Sugar Beet Co.	£2,750
1942	2654	*Cherwell*	Parkgate Iron & Steel Co. Ltd	£3,135
1942	2655	*Huntsmen*	Parkgate Iron & Steel Co. Ltd	£3,135
1942	2668	*Cranford No. 2*	Cranford Ironstone Co. Ltd	£3,344
1942	2670	*Lamport No. 3*	Staveley Coal & Iron Co. Ltd	£3,344
1942	2682	*No. 14 Princess*	Ribble Navigation	£3,750
1944	2860	*Birchenwood*	British Geco Eng.	£1,282
1950	2994	*Vulcan*	Steel Co. of Wales	£10,626
1951	2996	*Victor*	Steel Co. of Wales	£10,626
1953	3059	*No. 2 Florence*	National Coal Board	£10,127
1954	3061	*Empress*	National Coal Board	£10,302

3. Fireless Locos

0–4–0

1932	2473	No. 1	Huntly and Palmer	£1,440
1948	2898	*Patons*	Sir Alex Gibb & Partners	£4,433
1951	2989	*Huncoat No. 1*	British Electricity Authority	£5,365
1951	3022	*Huncoat No. 2*	British Electricity Authority	£7,229
1957	3121		English Clays Lovering Pochin Co.	£11,267

0–6–0

1929	2370		Distillers Co.	£1,830
1953	3019		Shell Refining Co.	£8,444

Total: 38

CHAPTER NINE

MODERNIZATION

Only three years after the opening of the new 'No. 5' signal-box in 1952, the Conservative government approved a capital expenditure of £1,240 million on the whole of the British railway system under the 1955 'Modernization Plan', to be spent on modern traction (less than a decade after BR had decided to persist with steam power), track reconstruction to overtake skimped maintenance of wartime years, resignalling and investment in freight handling. Plans for modernization of the West Coast main line were to bring dramatic change to the railway and station at Stafford as BR prepared to bring its system up to date in readiness for modern public demand for a fast, clean and efficient railway, steam locomotives being deemed dirty and outdated.

The station at Stafford, along with the railway serving the town, underwent significant change as a result of proposals under the 'Modernization Plan' which involved electrification of the LM Region's West Coast main line, including the Trent Valley line and the GJR from Stafford and through Wolverhampton (High Level), Birmingham (New Street) and Coventry to Rugby. Although the scheme had received state approval, it was to be surrounded by financial and political controversy throughout its construction programme, which caused delay and disruption for passengers using Stafford station.

Under the 'Modernization Plan' BR was to bring its railway system up to date by replacement of steam locomotives with new diesel and electric traction and substantial investment in the infrastructure, after years of neglect following the Second World War. Electrification of the East and West Coast main lines was envisaged, along with some areas in the Home Counties. The LM Region's line between Euston and the cities of Liverpool and Manchester, including the GJR line through Birmingham, was to be electrified at a cost of £118 million. These costs included substantial track improvements and completely new stations at Euston, Wolverhampton (High Level), Birmingham (New Street), Coventry and Stafford, as well as substantial refurbishments to many others, e.g. Manchester (London Road). All of this work was planned to be completed by 1964.

Work on electrification began in 1957 on the section between Crewe and Manchester, and in December 1957 the press announced that BR was to spend £5½ million over the next five or six years preparing track and infrastructure in the Stafford, Lichfield, Walsall and Wolverhampton areas for electrification. This included demolition and rebuilding of Stafford station, deep ballasting of track, and introduction of long welded rails. Work on Stafford station began in 1959.

By September 1960, the Crewe–Manchester section of electrification was complete, giving electric locos just enough mileage to demonstrate haulage,

Ex-LMS 'Princess Coronation' Pacific No. 46253 *City of St Albans*, in green livery, is leaving Stafford station with the Down *Red Rose* express from Euston to Liverpool, 3 May 1962. At this time electrification work around Stafford station was well under way, after the government had given permission for such work to continue in 1961. (*P. Kendrick; F.W. Shuttleworth Collection*)

acceleration and sustained speed capacity which were better than anything else BR could offer. However, on government orders, electrification on the West Coast main line was brought to a halt as costs had rocketed from £118 million to beyond £160 million, because of inflation and the cost of rebuilding bridges with enlarged clearances for the overhead wires, something not envisaged when the original plan had been drawn up. Not only had southward electrification been halted at Crewe, but a stop had been put on rebuilding Stafford station, which left the station half demolished and littered with builders' huts until the following spring when the government gave grudging approval to restart electrification work. The new Stafford station was given its official opening on 31 December 1962, only one week before electric services between Liverpool, Manchester, Crewe and Stafford began.

Another ex-LMS 'Princess Coronation' Pacific No. 46225 *Duchess of Gloucester*, passes the 1952 built No. 5 signal-box as it heads north with a Down express on 13 June 1962. The new Stafford station is under construction in the background and the new platforms can clearly be seen. Also in view is the new footbridge under construction, and the cranes in the distance are evidence that the new station buildings are also being erected. In only another six months the old station will have disappeared and the new one opened in its place. With delays to electrification work, steam power continued to be used on trains between Euston, Liverpool and Scotland right up to the early 1960s, with 'Princess Royal', 'Princess Coronation' and BR 'Britannia' Pacifics common at Stafford until the end of 1962. Their numbers, however, decreased when 'Modernization Plan' English-Electric Type 4 1Co–Co1 (later Class 40) diesel-electric locomotives took over from steam haulage on important Euston–Glasgow and Euston–Holyhead expresses as the 1960s dawned. Ex-LMS and BR 'Standard' 4–6–0s continued to work Birmingham trains, as well as secondary traffic and freights, until West Coast Main Line electrification was complete. New Diesel Multiple Unit trains took over from steam on local services between Stafford, Wolverhampton and Birmingham from 1956. (*G. Coltas*)

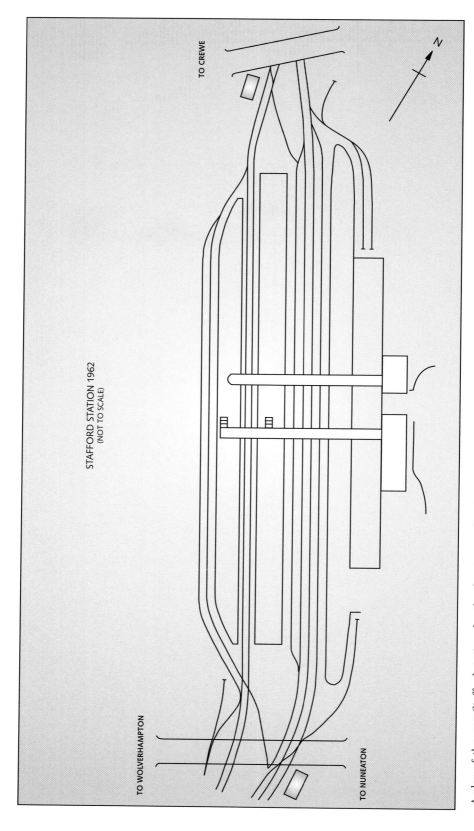

STAFFORD STATION 1962
(NOT TO SCALE)

TO CREWE

TO WOLVERHAMPTON

TO NUNEATON

N

A plan of the new Stafford station shortly after it opened in 1962. (*Author*)

The new Stafford station as it appeared when first opened. The new layout allowed separation of the London and Birmingham lines, which had been a bottleneck caused by crossover movements. To accommodate the separated Birmingham line, new through island platforms developed from old bays were built on the Down side of the station, these becoming platforms 4, 5 and 6, platform 6 being used by local electric services from Birmingham and Wolverhampton. The London tracks used the original platforms, Nos 1 and 3, with a pair of through lines for non-stop trains dividing the Up (No. 1) platform and Down (No. 3) platform lines. A bay platform, on the east side of platform 1, this being platform 2, was also provided. Beyond platform 6, running lines were provided to allow trains to bypass the station. Improvements were also made at Stafford Goods Yard, between the station and the start of the Trent Valley Line, to prevent shunting operations within the yard fouling the main lines. Newport Road bridge, adjacent to the east side of the station, was rebuilt to suit the new track layout and to give clearance for the overhead electric wires. Remodelling of the station meant that all former station buildings were demolished while the station remained open to passengers. Temporary buildings were provided for passengers and staff, making the place less comfortable while rebuilding was under way. The new station buildings were constructed in 1960s architects' favourite medium, concrete, and consisted of a main building which linked platform 1 with Station Road outside, a staff block carried on central columns at bridge level above platform 1, and waiting rooms on the island platforms. (*Author's Collection*)

Electric Stafford station in use, with 3,500 hp Bo-Bo electric locos hauling trains from December 1962. The still steam-hauled line from Stafford to Wellington was closed to passengers on 7 September 1964, any passengers for the Shropshire town having to go to Wolverhampton and change on to the old GWR route. From 1 August 1966 the section of the old LNWR line between Stafford and Newport was closed completely and subsequently lifted, following re-routing of freight trains via Bescot and Wolverhampton. Thus the line over which Captain Huish had fought so hard with the S&B was now just history. Electrification work beyond Stafford neared completion by the end of 1966 and all trains at Stafford became electric hauled. Diesel traction returned to Stafford from 1990, with the introduction of 'Inter-City 125' train sets following electrification of the East Coast Main Line, and they are still common on trains to the West Country, via Birmingham (New Street), and on services between Euston and Holyhead, these being operated by Virgin Trains following privatization of the railways from 1994. The station and its railway came under the control of the private Railtrack from 1 April 1994, and from 1997 Virgin Trains took control of the West Coast Main Line train services. Thus Stafford station is now in private hands, and with investment on the West Coast Main Line itself becoming a reality, its future seems assured. (*Author's Collection*)